WITHOUT A TRACE

20 BAFFLING MISSING PERSON
CASES FROM ACROSS AMERICA

JENN BAXTER

ISBN: 9798852288141

For Nana

CASES:

1. Edward & Stephania Andrews
2. Diamond Bynum & King Walker
3. Patricia Blough, Renee Bruhl, & Ann Miller
4. Joshua Guimond
5. Cleashindra Hall
6. Kelly Hollan
7. Kyron Horman
8. Sofia Juarez
9. Steven Koecher
10. Bianca LeBron
11. Melissa McGuinn
12. Kristen Modafferi
13. Morgan Nick
14. Leah Occhi
15. Timmothy Pitzen
16. Peggy Rahn & Wendy Stevenson
17. Kemberly Ramer
18. Jonathan Schaff
19. Brandon Swanson
20. Tabitha Tuders

Edward and Stephania Andrews

Edward Andrews and his wife, Stephania, were both 62 years old in 1970 and still had a very active social life. They had only been married for six years, and they owned a home together in Arlington Heights, a suburb of Chicago. Although they were both still working, they were planning on retiring at the end of the year and were looking forward to starting the next phase of their life.

May 15, 1970, started out as a routine Friday for the couple. They ate breakfast together at the dining room table and got ready to go to work. They both worked in Chicago; Edward was an executive with Miller-Peerless Manufacturing, and Stephania was a credit investigator for Local Loan. Each morning they made the commute to downtown Chicago in their 1969 Oldsmobile, taking the longer route along the lakefront because Edward disliked the high-speed driving necessary to negotiate the expressway.

Edward dropped Stephania off at her office and then continued to his job. The morning was uneventful, and Edward left his office at lunchtime to meet up with two of his friends, both executives with a company that Edward had worked at previously. They had planned to eat at Pizzeria Uno, a Chicago favorite, but Edward started to feel ill while they were at the restaurant and was unable to eat. One of the men he was having lunch with, E.J. Kreftmeyer, said that Edward had just lit a cigarette when he suddenly turned pale. He seemed to improve somewhat while they were sitting there, however, and even insisted on driving his two friends back to a nearby train station. Edward seemed to be fine on the short ride to the train station, and he made it back to his office with no problems.

Later that afternoon, one of Edward's employees noticed that he didn't look well. At one point, Edward folded his arms on his desk and laid his head down on them, something none of the employees had ever seen him do before. Once again, he seemed to recover fairly quickly. He left work at 5:00 pm and picked up his wife as usual.

The Andrews didn't go straight home after work that evening; they were going to a cocktail party that was being held at the Sheraton-Chicago Hotel. Stephania's supervisor had given her two tickets for the event, which was being sponsored by the Chicago chapter of the Women's Association of the Allied Beverage Industry.

The couple arrived at the party a little after 5:30 pm and began making their way through the crowd, stopping to chat with people that they knew. Edward seemed to have completely recovered from his earlier illness, and both he and Stephania appeared to be in a good mood. Neither of them was a heavy drinker, but they each enjoyed a couple of cocktails along with some of the canapes that were being passed around. Some of the guests at the party said that after a few hours, Edward looked as if he didn't feel well, and he was overheard complaining that he was hungry. His hunger made sense; he hadn't eaten any lunch that afternoon and there wasn't much food at the cocktail party.

Around 9:30 pm, he and Stephania left the party and headed for the hotel parking garage where they had left their car. Carl Peterson, the parking attendant, saw the couple when they stepped off the elevator and started walking towards their car. He was a bit surprised, as both Edward and Stephania seemed to be having trouble walking straight. He and the manager of the garage, Anthony Morelli, watched the couple closely as they struggled to get into the Oldsmobile. The garage employees were concerned, and Carl mentioned that he didn't think Edward should be driving. Edward started the car and waved dismissively at Carl, insisting he was fine to drive.

Edward put the car in gear and headed for the exit that was less than ten feet away. Anthony and Carl could only watch, dumbfounded, as he immediately drove the car directly into the side of the garage door. Anthony rushed over and examined the damage done to the door. Peering into the car, he told Edward that he was obviously in no condition to drive. Stephania, who was crying at this point, nodded in agreement. They begged Edward to get out of the car, but he refused to listen. He backed the car up, aligned it with the center of the garage door, and sped out of the garage.

The exit that Edward took led to Michigan Avenue, one of the main roads in the city. For several blocks on either side of the Chicago River, Michigan Avenue has two layers – the city used double- and triple-decker highways as a way of saving space – and when they left the parking garage, the Andrews would have been on the lower level. Anthony and Carl watched as the car turned south on Michigan Avenue and disappeared from view. It was the last time anyone would see Edward and Stephania.

It's unclear what happened to the Andrews after they left the cocktail party on Friday night, but they didn't make it back to their suburban home. The couple had no children – although one of Edward's previous wives had two children that he had adopted – and they had no weekend plans. It wasn't until Monday when they failed to show up at work that people began to realize that something was wrong. Both of them were conscientious employees who seldom missed work and would always call before taking any time off. Once it became clear that no one was able to get in contact with the couple, the police were called. Edward's sister, Helen Weller, was at a loss for words. Neither Edward nor Stephania was the type to go away without saying anything to someone.

Arlington Heights police were dispatched to the couple's home, but there was no sign of the couple. There were several newspapers piled up on their front lawn, and it looked like they hadn't checked their mailbox for several days. A neighbor who had a spare key to their house unlocked the door for the police, unsure what to expect once they got inside. The house was quiet and appeared to be empty. The fact that there were still some plates and grapefruit rinds on the dining room table led investigators to believe the pair had never made it home from the cocktail party.

Except for the dishes, which Stephania had probably planned to take care of when she got home Friday, there was nothing out of place in the house and no indication that any kind of struggle had taken place. Investigators noted that Stephania's cosmetics and jewelry were in the home, and Edward's shavings supplies were as well. Coupled with the fact that none of their clothes appeared to be missing, police took this to mean that the pair hadn't simply taken off on an impromptu vacation. They had no idea what had happened to Edward and Stephania, but they were pretty sure that the answer wasn't going to be found in the home.

Investigators began interviewing family, friends, and colleagues of the couple, trying to get a better understanding of what was going on when the pair went missing. Friends said that the couple seemed to have a good marriage, and there were no problems that anyone was aware of. They were both very neat and orderly, and they took pride in their appearance and their home. Even one of Edward's ex-wives had nothing but good things to say about him, telling investigators he was responsible and conscientious; certainly not the kind of man who would abandon his job. They weren't wealthy, but they were comfortable. Some of their neighbors said that they barely knew the couple, but would often see them leaving their home all dressed up so they assumed that they attended lots of parties. It was an accurate assumption. They loved to socialize and often went out to various events, although they also enjoyed entertaining people in their home.

Oddly enough, it was Edward's own sister who injected some drama into the case, insinuating that Edward had been keeping secrets from people. Stephania and her family were under the impression that Edward had been married four times in the past, but his sister claimed that the real number was more like six or seven. Even odder, she refused to clarify the exact number and provided no proof of these allegations. Regardless, it didn't look like any of Edward's ex-wives had anything to do with his disappearance.

It soon became clear that no one had any contact with Edward or Stephania after they left the cocktail party on Friday evening. As far as the detectives could determine, the two men who had been working in the parking garage had been the last to see the couple, and their description of what had taken place was disturbing. They were able to positively identify the couple from pictures that the police showed them; they were absolutely certain that Stephania and Edward were the couple that they had witnessed staggering in the parking garage before slamming into the garage door and taking off on Michigan Avenue. But relatives and friends of the couple were just as certain that the garage employees were mistaken. They were not heavy drinkers, and they had not been displaying any signs of intoxication when they left the cocktail party. Edward was also very particular about his cars. If he had hit something, his friends said that he would have immediately jumped out to inspect the damage. Without surveillance cameras, there was no way police could be absolutely certain that the staggering couple had been Edward and Stephania, but they believed that it had been them. The garage employees had accurately described the couple and their Oldsmobile.

Some of the people who had been at the cocktail party told investigators that Edward had looked as if he wasn't feeling well shortly before leaving the hotel. Edward's coworkers, as well as the two friends he had gone to lunch with, were able to provide more details. They raised the possibility that perhaps Edward had a heart attack that evening, and the ill feelings he had experienced throughout the day had been warning signs that he failed to pay attention to. Until Edward was located, there was no way they could know for sure, but it certainly seemed like something was going on with his health that day. They knew that the couple had made it back to their car that evening, and there was nothing in their home to indicate that they had returned there after the cocktail party. Whatever had happened to them, it looked as if it happened to them while they were on the road.

It was possible that the couple had run into car trouble, so Investigators began going over every possible route the couple could have taken home. Helicopters assisted in the search from the air, carefully checking for any evidence that could indicate their car had skidded off the road, and flying over parking lots looking for the missing Oldsmobile. No one could find any sign of the couple or their car.

The two garage employees had told police that Edward had headed north on the lower level of Michigan Avenue when he exited the garage, but there was some speculation that, in his confused state, he may have gotten into the southbound lane. Heading the wrong way down the highway would have put them at risk of having a head-on collision, but there were no accidents reported that night. If Edward had realized he was going the wrong way, he would have had to wait until he got off the bridge over the Chicago River before he would have been able to do a U-turn. Investigators did find a couple of areas on East Wacker Drive, which crossed Michigan Avenue right near the bridge, where there was enough space in the guardrail for a car to potentially drive through. They could tell from scrape marks on the guardrail that they had been hit more than once in the past, but there were also some tire prints that seemed to be fairly recent. The Chicago Police Department dragged the river near that location but found nothing.

Investigators would eventually drag the river in several different spots but they found no trace of the missing couple or their car. The river was only around 16 feet deep in the areas where a car could have ended up, and there were no strong currents. Police believed that if their car had ended up on the river, it would have quickly sunk down to the riverbed in the same general area where it entered the river. After their attempts to locate the car there were unsuccessful, some of the investigators believed that meant the car had not ended up in the Chicago River. But if they weren't in the river, where were they? It was hard to believe that two adults – and a car – could vanish without leaving a single clue behind.

Investigators considered the possibility that Edward and Stephania had been the victims of a robbery attempt that went horribly wrong. The couple did not usually carry a large amount of cash with them, but they did have 13 or 14 different credit cards. Police monitored them for any activity, but neither their bank account nor any of their credit cards were touched. Their bank statements showed that the couple normally left most of their money in the bank, and they hadn't made any unusual withdrawals in the two months leading up to the disappearance, a fact which made it very unlikely that the pair had decided to just run off and begin a new life somewhere else. If they were still alive, they weren't spending any of their money.

Detectives weren't sure what jurisdiction the couple had gone missing from, so both the Arlington Heights Police Department and the Chicago Police Department were working on the case. But even with their combined skills, the investigation soon stalled. There were no reported sightings of the couple, and still no trace of their car. They had ruled out the idea that the pair had voluntarily left, and they didn't have any evidence that foul play was involved. They believed that the most likely explanation was that the couple had been involved in a tragic accident, but they still hadn't been able to determine where. Time and again, the detectives returned to the river. It seemed to be the most logical explanation; it was only a block from the hotel where the cocktail party had been held, and if Edward had been as sick as people had described, the investigators couldn't imagine him

12

getting very far. It had taken him two tries to get the car out of the parking garage. If he had misjudged how much room he had to make a U-turn off the bridge, he wouldn't have gotten a second chance.

In April of 1971, police searched the river yet again, this time with sonar equipment. They hoped that the new equipment would be able to detect something that they had missed in early searches, but it yielded the same frustrating result. In November of 1971, they obtained more sophisticated sonar equipment and performed yet another search. Once again, they were unsuccessful in finding anything related to the missing couple. They still felt that the river held the answers they were looking for, but after failing to find anything useful, they forced themselves to move on and consider different options. A search team went and dredged a pond in Des Plaines, Illinois after someone suggested that the couple and their car could have ended up there. They did find three cars in the pond, but none of them were the Oldsmobile they were so desperately seeking. They were out of leads, and the case soon went cold.

For the most part, the case dropped from the headlines. Edward and Stephania, along with their 1969 Oldsmobile, seemed to literally vanish without a trace. Local newspapers would usually publish a short recap of the case each year on the anniversary of the couple's disappearance, and this would often result in a couple of tips being called in to the detectives, but they usually led nowhere. By the mid-1980s, there was a movement to revitalize downtown Chicago. In addition to all the work that was being done on roads and buildings, the city also decided to do a general cleaning of the Chicago River. It was a massive undertaking. In addition to the tons of trash, bottles, and abandoned shopping carts that were found, the cleanup crews also discovered cars in the river – 12 cars – but once again, there was no sign of the Oldsmobile. The Chicago River had been the focal point of the Andrews investigation for so long; if the river held the answers to the mysterious disappearance, it was keeping them well hidden.

By 1994, there were many people living in Chicago who had never heard of Edward and Stephania Andrews. The detectives who had originally worked on the case were retired, and the case hadn't been mentioned in any newspaper for years. But for the relatives of the missing couple, the pain had never gone away. They were certain that the pair were long dead, but they had never stopped hoping that they would someday get to give them a proper burial. Suddenly, in July of 1994, it looked like they might finally get some closure. A 36-year-old man, only 12 at the time the couple went missing, went to law enforcement and told them that he knew what had happened to Edward and Stephania. The detectives were skeptical but listened to what the man had to say.

The man claimed that the couple had been killed on the night that they had gone missing, and their bodies had been put in the trunk of their car and submerged in a pond near Green Oaks, Illinois. He blamed the murders on a group of young men that liked to cause trouble in the city in the 1970s, and he claimed that he had been at the pond the night they disposed of the car there. When he was asked why he had waited more than two decades to come forward with this information, he told the investigators that he had been stricken with amnesia. At that point, they were pretty certain that his story wasn't going to hold up, but it was the first lead they'd gotten about the case in years.

Investigators quietly reopened the case and began

trying to verify the information that the young man had given them. There were parts of his story that didn't make any sense, but there were enough verifiable facts included that they decided to search the pond in question. A group of police officers and firefighters began the process of searching through the pond, and they did locate something buried in the muck at the bottom of the pond, but they were unable to determine what it was and didn't have the equipment necessary to do a full-blown salvage operation. They marked the location of the object, about 10 feet from the edge of the pond. The search was called off while investigators made arrangements for Roger Chapman, a salvage expert from Milwaukee, to come out to the location. Roger was considered one of the best, and he and his company had successfully located submerged airplanes and more than 50 sunken ships. He spent two hours in the water with a police diver before determining that, though there was some metal in the pond, the object was definitely not a car. Although the investigators were disappointed, they hadn't been all that confident about the man's information to begin with. It was harder for Edward and Stephania's relatives, as their hopes for answers were once again dashed.

The pond search would be the last push to find the remains of the couple. The investigation is no longer considered active; both Edward and Stephania would be over 110 years old now, so there is no chance that they are still alive.

Edward Andrews was 62 years old when he vanished from Chicago, Illinois in May 1970. His wife, Stefania, was also 62 years old at the time. Due to the length of time since their disappearance, detectives know they will not be found alive but would still like to know what happened to them. If you have any information about the fate of Edward and Stephania or the whereabouts of their 1969 Oldsmobile, please contact the Arlington Heights Police Department at 847-368-5300.

Diamond Bynum and King Walker

Diamond Bynum was born with Prader-Willi Syndrome, a genetic disorder characterized by slow mental development, short stature, and unceasing hunger. The 21-year-old had the mental capacity of a 7-year-old, but maintained a bubbly personality and an infectious smile. She was in an especially excited mood on July 25, 2015. Her father, Eugene, was celebrating his birthday the following day, and it was a family tradition that Diamond received a few gifts of her own whenever any family member had a birthday. On this occasion, she had asked for scented soaps and chocolate milk; her grandmother had already purchased both and planned on giving them to her the following day.

Diamond lived in Gary, Indiana with her father and stepmother. Her 2-year-old nephew, King Walker, was also staying with them on this particular Saturday; her stepmother, Suzanne, was babysitting the toddler while his mother was attending a class in Chicago. Midway through the morning, Suzanne put King down for a nap, and Diamond fell asleep with him. At some point, Suzanne also drifted off. It's unclear exactly what happened while she was asleep, but she woke up to a nightmare. Diamond and King were missing.

As soon as Suzanne realized that Diamond and King were not in the house, she rushed outside, frantically scanning the streets for any sign of them. She expected to see them nearby, but the streets were empty and Suzanne started to panic. King was a typical toddler – he loved to run – but Diamond's genetic condition meant that she was quite overweight, walked with a limp, and was not one to wander too far from home. To make matters worse, the family had just moved to Gary a few months before. Prior to this, they had lived in Hammond, Indiana. Diamond knew the streets and people of Hammond well, and it was impossible for her to get lost there because a neighbor would guide her home if they saw her outside. Here in Gary, Diamond didn't know her way around and didn't really know any of the neighbors. Worried, Suzanne called Eugene at work. He immediately came home, and after making another cursory search of the surrounding area, the couple called police and reported Diamond and King missing.

Eugene believed that King had likely woken up from his nap first, and had decided he wanted to go outside. This would have prompted Diamond to get up and follow him outside. Diamond liked to think of herself as King's babysitter, though she was always supervised herself and never left alone with the toddler. King's current favorite game was to run around and make people chase him. If Diamond had followed him more than a few houses away in any direction, she may have become disoriented and unable to find her way home. Her genetic condition made it hard for her to communicate with people, and King knew only a few words, he couldn't speak in full sentences yet. If they needed help, it was going to be exceedingly difficult for them to get people to understand what they were saying.

Police started their search by going door-to-door on the streets surrounding the Bynum's home. Flyers were handed out with descriptions of Diamond and King, and residents were interviewed. No one recalled seeing the pair that day. Family members visited area businesses and hung up missing posters in every window possible. Employees at a nearby McDonald's were the first to report a positive sighting of Diamond and King – but the two had been sighted in McDonald's before they had been reported missing, so the employees had simply given them food and watched them go on their way.

All the restaurants and food stores in the area were told to be on the lookout for the missing pair. Diamond's Prader-Willi Syndrome caused her to feel ravenously hungry all the time – while living in Hammond, she had been known to take food off store shelves and hide in the bathroom to eat – so it seemed likely she would head for places where she could get a snack. As darkness descended with no sign of Diamond or King, fear began to set in. Eugene began to worry that someone had abducted his daughter and grandson.

Due to the fact that Diamond was technically an adult, the criteria to issue an Amber Alert was not met in this case. While the family became convinced that someone must have taken the missing pair, police were not quick to embrace this theory. There was nothing to indicate an abduction had taken place – no one witnessed them being forced into a car, and the McDonald's employees were adamant that there had been no third party with them at the restaurant. But if they hadn't been abducted, where were they?

If Diamond and King were still in the area, it seemed impossible they could go unnoticed for any length of time. Missing posters were plastered on every available surface. The National Center for Missing and Exploited Children placed billboards with their pictures on local highways. A mass text message containing information about the missing pair was sent to every cell number in the area. Yet nothing brought police any closer to finding them.

Gary, Indiana is rife with abandoned buildings and closed storefronts – there are more than 15,000 of them throughout the city. On Wednesday, the Indiana Department of Homeland Security assisted the Gary Police Department in searching those buildings closest to the Bynum home with K9 units. The city was experiencing a heatwave, and it was possible that Diamond, unable to find her way home, had sought shelter somewhere out of the sun. One by one, over the next three days, each building in a 24-block area was thoroughly searched. There were no signs of Diamond or King.

The search seemed to lose momentum at this point. Everyone involved with the case knew there was no way Diamond was capable of taking care of herself – let alone a toddler – for any length of time. The fact that they hadn't been found indicated to police that they were either no longer in the area or someone had taken them in and was keeping them hidden. Police started looking into registered sex offenders in the area. There were 21 living within a mile of the Bynum home, a fact which shocked and horrified Eugene. The thought that one of them might have gotten ahold of his daughter and grandson was almost too much to bear.

In the middle of August, police named a person of interest in the case, a 34-year-old local man. Diamond and King's loved ones held their breath, hoping that answers were in sight. It took police a couple of weeks to locate and interview the man, but they eventually said the man was no longer a suspect. Police were back to square one, and it was a letdown for the family.

With all local leads seemingly exhausted, police, with the help of other agencies, began expanding the search outside of the Gary city limits. A Silver Alert was issued for Diamond and King; police believed Diamond was likely in need of medical attention as she was without her prescription medication. Many questioned why this hadn't been done sooner, and no real answer was offered as to why police waited until the end of August to request the Silver Alert.

As months passed by, public interest in the case waned and the disappearance fell out of the headlines. Police said the case remained active, but no new leads had been called in and they were no closer to learning what had happened to Diamond and King. The family tried to remain positive, and they continued to search through abandoned buildings on their own time. Eugene was unwavering in his belief that the two were still alive, bolstered by the fact that no bodies had been found. Still, as the holidays approached, he noted that the family had little to celebrate. He just wanted his family back together again.

Months turned to years, and the case grew colder. In October 2016, the Northwest Indiana Major Crimes Task Force announced that they were going to take another look at the disappearance of Diamond and King. They spent a week at the Gary Police Department's headquarters, where they combed through all the files on the case. In addition to re-interviewing people in the neighborhood and conducting searches with K9 units, they also submitted several items to the Indiana State Police crime lab for further testing. They had high hopes of breathing new life into the case, but by 2018 the case had grown cold once again.

There are several theories about what might have happened to Diamond and King, but little evidence to back up any of them. Early in the case, the Bynum family saw the dark side of social media when people began to accuse them of being responsible for the disappearance. It's important to note that police have never insinuated that anyone in the family has ever been a suspect in this case.

Others have speculated that Diamond may have been talking to someone online who was then responsible for harming her and King. While Diamond did have access to a tablet and a cell phone, both of them were left behind when she went missing and it appears she used them mostly for playing games. Eugene posted online that his daughter didn't know how to read; so it is highly unlikely she was communicating with anyone on the internet.

At this point, police believe that the only way they are going to solve the case is with the public's help. They believe someone out there knows what happened to Diamond and King on that hot July day in 2015, and they hope anyone with information will come forward so they can finally provide closure for Diamond and King's family.

Diamond Bynum was just 21 years old when she went missing from Gary, Indiana in July 2015. Diamond has brown eyes and black hair that had gold highlights in it, and at the time of her disappearance, she was 4 feet 8 inches tall and weighed 240 pounds. She was last seen wearing a white shirt and either blue or purple pants. Due to Prader-Willi Syndrome, she is constantly hungry and may try to steal food; cheeseburgers are her favorite. King Walker was just 2 years old when he went missing with Diamond. He has brown eyes and black hair, and at the time of his disappearance, he was 3 feet tall and weighed 34 pounds. He was last seen wearing a blue shirt and red shorts. If you have any information about Diamond and King, please contact the Gary Police Department at 219-881-1260.

Patricia Blough, Renee Bruhl, and Ann Miller

Summers in Chicago tend to be very hot and muggy, and the summer of 1966 was no exception. Looking for a way to beat the oppressive heat, three young women decided to spend Saturday, July 2nd at Indiana Dunes State Park. Eager to get the holiday weekend started, 21-year-old Ann Miller left her house early that morning to pick up her two friends. Her first stop was 19-year-old Patricia Blough's house. Patty had been watching for the familiar sight of Ann's 1955 Buick and she ran out the door as soon as Ann pulled up to her house. She yelled a quick goodbye to her mother, telling her that she would be back early. Renee Bruhl, the third girl of the trio, was married and needed to be home in time to cook dinner for her husband, so Patty told her mother to expect her home around 5:00 pm. The two girls made the short drive to the west side of Chicago to pick up 19-year-old Renee, and by 8:00 am they left the city and headed for the Dunes.

They arrived at the park around 10:00 am. The beach was packed with people looking forward to enjoying the long holiday weekend, but the girls took little notice of the crowd. They spread their blanket out about 100 yards away from the shore, choosing a spot close to a few poplar trees that would provide a little bit of shade from the relentless sun. Though it was still early, the temperature had already topped 90 degrees and would continue to climb for the next few hours. The girls stripped down to their bathing suits and settled themselves on the blanket, content to just relax and soak in the atmosphere for a while.

Like Ann, Patty, and Renee, Mike Yankalasa and Frances Cicero also lived in Chicago. The teenage couple had also decided to join the crowd at the Dunes that Saturday, and they had staked out a spot in the sand that was close to where the three girls were. Around noon, they watched as the trio got up and began to make the 100-yard walk to the water's edge. Although the teenagers hadn't really been paying much attention to the girls, they couldn't help but notice that they had left all of their belongings – purses, wallets, a radio, and everything else they had brought – unattended on their beach blanket. It didn't strike Mike and Frances as a very smart thing to do, but they figured it wasn't any of their business. Obviously the three girls trusted that no one would steal anything while they were gone. They were probably just going to take a quick dip in the water to cool off and then come right back.

Mike and Frances continued to lay out in their little spot of sand, idly watching the crowds of people sunbathing and swimming. It was common to see small boats pulling up close to the shoreline, almost all of them piloted by good-looking young men. These men would hone in on a group of pretty women, maneuver closer, and try to entice them to take a boat ride. The teenage couple watched in amusement as three young men pulled their boat close to where Ann, Patty, and Renee were, and though they couldn't hear any snippets of conversation from where they were sitting, it was obvious that the men were trying to talk them into getting on their boat. The women weren't impressed, and the men soon gave up and went off in search of more amiable targets. It wasn't long before a man in a smaller boat moved in towards the three girls, and Mike and Frances exchanged amused glances.

The three women sure seemed to be popular with the guys. Their amusement quickly turned to surprise, though, as they watched the three girls climb up into the boat. Once they had settled in, the boat sailed off to the west and the teenagers lost sight of it. They thought it was odd that the women would sail away with all of their belongings still sitting on the beach, but there was little use in dwelling on it. They had come to the beach to have fun, not to sit around worrying about the possessions of three women that they didn't even know.

As the sun began to set, the crowd on the beach finally started to thin out. Crowds of tired, sunburned people made their way to the parking lot and tried to remember where they had left their cars. Mike and Frances joined the crowd heading for the parking lot, but as they got closer to where they had been sitting earlier in the day, they saw something that made them stop in their tracks. It appeared that the three women hadn't made it back from their boat ride yet. Their beach blanket and all their belongings were still in the exact spot where they had left them so many hours earlier. The teenagers stood there for a minute, uncertain of what to do. They saw a park ranger walking nearby, so they flagged him over and told him about the three women who had left on a boat around noon and not come back for their things. They had no idea who the women were, but they were able to describe them as well as the boat they had seen them getting into.

Bud Conner had been a park ranger for years, and he was used to dealing with situations like this. The women had probably decided to go on an afternoon picnic that had turned into a moonlit cruise. Bud thanked the teenagers and told them he would put everything in the park office so that it would be safe until the women returned. Picking the blanket up by its corners, he checked to make sure that nothing had been missed and then carried everything to the Park Superintendent William Svetic's office. It certainly wasn't the first time someone had left something behind on the beach. They would probably get a call from the women in the morning, and they would be pleased to know that their possessions were safe.

Sunday was another busy day at the Dunes. The holiday weekend was in full swing, and the park rangers had their hands full dealing with the crowd of people. Monday was July 4th, and the rangers arrived that morning expecting another busy and crowded day at the state park. William had just unlocked his office when he got a phone call from a man who identified himself as Harold Blough. He told the park superintendent that he was trying to locate his daughter. She had gone to the Dunes on Saturday with two friends but had never come home. He was trying to determine if there had been an accident or anything else that might explain what had happened to the three young women.

William had forgotten all about the belongings that Bud had brought to the office on Saturday night, but as he was speaking with Harold he checked and saw that the blanket was still in his office. A quick check confirmed that the car keys found on the blanket were to a 1955 Buick that was still sitting in the parking lot, but the women were nowhere to be found. It was only 8:50 am, but it was clear this wasn't going to be a routine day at the park. Suspecting he was dealing with something far more serious than some forgotten belongings, William called the Indiana State Police.

Indiana State Trooper Harry Young was the first officer on the scene. The first thing he did was call in the license plate number of the Buick. It didn't take long for him to determine that there had been a missing person report filed on the owner of the Buick and two of her friends, all of whom had been missing since Saturday. Trooper Young confirmed that Ann's car had been found, but there was no sign of the women. Sergeant Edward Burke, a state police detective, was the next officer to arrive at the scene. He inventoried all the items that the women had left on the beach, as well as those that were still in the car. In addition to leaving their purses and wallets behind, it soon became clear that the women had left their clothing and shoes behind as well. Wherever the women went, they were barefoot and clad only in their bathing suits.

The first 48 hours of an investigation are always the most critical, but the women had been missing since Saturday. Police had already lost those crucial first hours and couldn't afford to waste any time in getting the investigation started. Sgt. Burke immediately requested that the Coast Guard begin a search of the lake while he interviewed employees and anyone else who may have seen the women that Saturday. Unfortunately, there wasn't a lot to go on. The beach had been crowded, and none of the employees recalled speaking with the three women. The teenagers who spoke to Bud had told him that the women got on a small white boat that had a blue interior and an outboard motor. They had estimated it to be around 14 feet long. According to the Coast Guard, there had been more than 5000 boats on the lake between Chicago and the park that Saturday; isolating the one that the women had boarded was an impossible task.

The couple who had witnessed the women getting on the boat described the boat's pilot as a tanned man in his 20s with dark, wavy hair. They could tell he had a life jacket on, but that was all they had been able to observe. Family members of the women told investigators that, as far as they knew, the women didn't know anyone who owned a boat, but they also believed that the women wouldn't have gone with someone they didn't know.

Search parties began the grueling task of going over every inch of the 2180-acre park. It was one of the most extensive manhunts the state of Indiana had ever seen. In addition to the beach and the lake, there were many wooded areas and open fields in the state park. With no way of knowing if the women had gone missing on the lake or after they were brought back to shore, police knew they needed to search each section of the park. The teenagers said that the boat that the women got on had headed to the west, so search parties were sent off in that direction first. On Wednesday, debris from a boat washed up on the shore about three miles from where the women had last been seen. Civil Air Patrol planes flew over the area, but no other debris was spotted. Coast Guard cruisers began checking every boat along the Lake Michigan shoreline, covering areas in Indiana, Michigan, and Illinois. Dozens of scuba divers scoured the lake, volunteers with bloodhounds covered every inch of accessible land, and a steady stream of helicopters and planes flew over the search area. There were many privately owned cabins along the lakeside, and the police asked the owners to look around their property for any sign of the missing women.

It didn't take long for the media to pick up on the story of the three missing girls, and their pictures made the front page of newspapers around the country. While the publicity helped to generate many tips, most involved purported sightings of the women that police were unable to confirm. Boaters who had been on the lake that

Saturday told investigators that they had seen the women in water up to their chins, and police wondered if perhaps the women had just gone out too far and had drowned. But all three women were strong swimmers, and it was hard to imagine that three people would have been able to drown without any of the lifeguards on duty noticing a thing.

Detectives got their first break in the case when a man came forward and told them he had been shooting home videos at the lake the day the women had gone missing. Although he didn't remember seeing the trio, he told police that they were welcome to go through his videos if they thought it would help in the investigation. Police took him up on his offer, hoping that the videos would help them in their search for the boat that the women had gotten on. They were lucky; the video showed three women getting onto a small white boat that had a distinctive three-hulled design. Although it was hard to make out their faces on the video, the three women were wearing swimsuits that matched the descriptions of what Ann, Renee, and Patty had been wearing, and the male that was piloting the boat matched the description given by witnesses. It appeared that Patty sat at the front of the boat with the male, and the other two girls sat in the seats behind them. The boat could be seen heading to the west before it disappeared from the video.

Police were certain they had been able to pinpoint the boat that had picked up the three women, but they still had no idea whose boat it was or where it might be. There was also a chance that the boat hadn't been at all involved in the women's disappearance. It was possible that the women had returned safely from their boat ride only to have something happen to them later in the day. Some witnesses claimed that the small boat had dropped the women off at a beach to the west of where they had left all their belongings. An attorney and his wife were certain they had seen the women getting something to eat and wandering around the dunes before being picked up by a cabin cruiser with three men aboard. There was some speculation that the man who had been piloting the small white boat had dropped the women off on the western beach and then came back for them later, this time in the larger cabin cruiser with two of his friends. It was certainly possible that the women had been dropped off on the western beach, but police didn't have enough evidence to prove or disprove this theory. It seems unlikely that the women would have been seen getting something to eat, however, as all of their money had been left on their beach blanket.

After a week of intensive searching, officials were confident that the women were not anywhere in the state park. Every inch of the park had been searched without finding any trace of the women. They were also certain that the women hadn't drowned, as their bodies would have surfaced by that point. Once they had ruled out accidental drowning, police were left with two main theories about what might have happened. Either the women had run into foul play after accepting a boat ride with an unknown person, or they had staged their own disappearance. Their families insisted that there was no way the young women would have voluntarily walked away from their families, but police weren't so sure. As the focus of the investigation shifted to the personal lives of the three women, investigators grew more convinced that they were dealing with a voluntary disappearance.

Renee and Patty had been classmates and friends for years. They got to know Ann because she and Patty both boarded their horses at the Tricolor Stables in

Palatine, Illinois. The three women had bonded over their mutual love of horses and would often ride together. On the surface, their horseback riding seemed to be a wholesome pastime, but as detectives soon learned, there were some sinister undertones. Tricolor Stables was owned by George Jayne. Both George and his half-brother Silas Jayne had been involved in various fraudulent activities and police were quite familiar with the pair. Police were certain that Silas had orchestrated the murder of three young boys in 1955, but they were never able to come up with the evidence needed to charge him and they suspected that George had helped him cover it up. While they may have been involved in mutual criminal activities, George and Silas were not close and there was a long-standing feud between the two of them.

In June of 1965, an incident at Tricolor Stables illustrated just how serious the feud had become. George's Cadillac was blocking the entrance to the stables, and a young woman named Cheryl Ann Rude had been sent out to move it. As soon as she started the engine, the car blew up. There was no doubt that George had been the intended target, and he was sure that Silas had been behind the bombing. The incident made him so paranoid that he devised a way to start a car while standing outside the passenger side door. After Ann, Patty, and Renee went missing, there were whispers that perhaps one or more of the women had witnessed the car bomb being planted and they were killed because of it. But the bombing incident had taken place more than a year before the women went missing, and it seems unlikely that someone would have waited that long before ensuring their silence.

While Silas and George Jayne may not have been directly responsible for the women's disappearance, the connection between the man and the three women couldn't be denied. When police took an inventory of the items that the women had left behind, they discovered the phone numbers for both George Jayne and Silas Jayne's wife. The women knew what the men were capable of doing, and it's quite possible that they were afraid of the men. But were they scared enough to run away and go into hiding? A couple of months before the women vanished, Patty came home with an extremely bruised and swollen face. She told her family that she had an accident while horseback riding, but it was obvious to her friends that the injury had come from a fist, not a fall. When her friends asked her about it, she told them that she was having trouble with some "horse syndicate" people. She didn't elaborate, but her friends were sure that at least one of the Jayne brothers was to blame. Perhaps the women realized that they were in over their heads and believed that disappearing was the safest course of action.

The three women would often go to a tavern together after they had been horseback riding, and there was some speculation that Ann and Patty had become involved with a couple of married men who would frequent the same tavern. Ann had mentioned to some of her friends that she was three months pregnant in July of 1966, though she didn't have a steady boyfriend and her family didn't know anything about it. Apparently, she mentioned to some of her friends that she was thinking about going to a home for unwed mothers. After the women went missing, there were rumors that Patty had gotten pregnant as well, though there is no factual evidence to back this up.

While unwed mothers have become fairly common in today's world, this was not the case in 1966. If one of the women had become pregnant, she risked the possibility of being shunned by her family and shamed by others. With no legal options available for terminating a pregnancy, she faced a tough decision. She could enter a home for unwed mothers, knowing that her child would be branded with the stigma of illegitimacy, or she could risk her own life and get an illegal abortion, most likely in a less-than-sterile environment. Was it possible that an illegitimate pregnancy was the catalyst for the women's disappearance?

Dick Wylie was a reporter in Chicago when the women went missing, and he covered the disappearance extensively. Although he went on to become a police officer in Florida, he returned to Chicago after he retired and spent years researching this case. The amount of time that had passed made it impossible to know for certain what happened on that hot summer day, but Dick came up with several theories that he believed would explain why the women disappeared. Initially, Dick believed that at least one of the women had arranged to have an illegal abortion done on that day, only to have something go horribly wrong. According to Dick, there was a husband and wife team, Helen and Frank Largo, who operated an illegal abortion mill on a houseboat somewhere in the waters of Lake Michigan. He believed that the man seen piloting the boat that the women got in was most likely Ralph Largo, the couple's nephew, and that he was the one responsible for shuttling the women to the larger boat where the abortion would be performed. Dick thought that a botched abortion resulted in the death of one of the women, and the other two may have been killed so that there would be no witnesses.

There were several problems with this theory, however, the first being a complete lack of evidence to back it up. Even Dick admitted that unless further evidence – like a body – turned up, it would be impossible to prove what had happened. It seemed unlikely that the women would have left all of their belongings on the beach if they knew they would be leaving the immediate area on a boat. Dick believed that the women would have been comfortable leaving their purses behind, knowing that they would be returning in 90 minutes or so, but this seems unlikely. Most women wouldn't be comfortable leaving their purses unattended for the few minutes it would take to run to the ladies' room; it's unreasonable to think that the women would have left them behind on the beach while they went off to visit an abortion clinic in the middle of a lake. If the women had known ahead of time that they would have been taking a boat ride, it's likely that they would have chosen to keep their purses and wallets locked inside Ann's car.

Dick Wylie also considered that the women may have voluntarily disappeared. There were some credible sightings of the women in Michigan after they went missing, and the women's behavior in the weeks leading up to the disappearance made it appear that there were some things they were trying to hide from their families. Patty made several trips to the Dunes that summer. On one occasion, she agreed to let her brother accompany her to the park but then left in the morning without waking him up. When he questioned her about it later, she told him that he wouldn't have wanted to go since she and her friends had met some guys while they were there. There's no way to prove it now, but it's possible that the women had visited the park in order to finalize their plans for running away.

If the women had decided to stage their own disappearance, it would explain why they had left all of their belongings on the beach – they wanted people to think that they were dead. None of their relatives believed that the women would have voluntarily disappeared, but they also didn't know about some of the things that had been going on in the women's lives. They were aware that the women liked to go horseback riding together and would often meet at Tricolor Stables, but they had no idea about any of the criminal activity that was going on there. The girls were young when they started going to the stables, and they may have found some of the criminal undertones to be quite exciting at first. While they may have seen flirting with married men in bars as just some innocent fun, eventually they would have heard rumors about the heavy criminal activity that the men were involved in. Allegations of drug use, murder, and the killing of show horses for insurance money would have been hard to ignore, and it appeared that Patty had been roughed up on at least one occasion. Could this have been the catalyst that led to the women deciding they needed to escape somehow? It's certainly a possibility.

Despite the fact that the families of the missing women were insistent that the women were not the type to run away, each woman did have some issues in their personal life that may have driven them to disappear. Ann was rumored to be pregnant, and that alone would have been reason enough for her to contemplate running away. Patty had alluded to getting into some trouble with "horse syndicate" people, and may have concluded that the only way to escape the situation she found herself in was to simply disappear. Renee appeared to be happily married, but detectives made an interesting discovery when they were inventorying the items she had left behind in her purse. In a letter addressed to her husband, Renee wrote that she was unhappy with her marriage and was contemplating getting a divorce. She accused her husband of spending far too much time building hot rod cars with his friends and not paying any attention to her. Her husband told investigators that he didn't think they had been having any marital problems and he was confused by the letter. Her family was also unaware of any problems in the relationship. Renee had never bothered to mail the letter, and it's possible that she had written it while in a fit of rage and had forgotten all about it after she calmed down.

Perhaps the best argument against the women staging their own disappearance is the fact that none of them ever contacted anyone in their families. Adults go voluntarily missing all the time, but it's extremely rare for them to never be heard from again. If the women felt that events going on in their lives that summer necessitated them running away, it's reasonable to assume that they would have reached out to their relatives once those issues had been taken care of. George Jayne was shot to death in 1970, and Silas was found guilty of conspiracy in his brother's murder and sent to prison. If the women had disappeared in an attempt to hide from the brothers, they likely would have come out of hiding once both brothers were out of the picture.

It's also possible that the horse industry and its criminal connections had absolutely nothing to do with the disappearance of the three women. Although it would still be several years before Ted Bundy would capture the attention of the nation and make serial killers a household name, such killers did exist and there's always a chance that the women were unfortunate enough to cross paths with one. The man who was piloting the boat that picked the women up has never been identified, and it's unknown if he had anything to do with the disappearance or not. So many years have passed that it's possible there is no one still alive today that knows just what happened to the three women. Unless the bodies of the women are found or the killer decides to come forward, the truth may never be discovered.

The women are still listed as missing persons, although police know that it is highly unlikely that any of them are still alive. The case file is still reviewed periodically, and investigators remain hopeful that they will one day learn just what happened on that hot summer day more than 55 years ago to turn a routine trip to the beach into one of Indiana's most baffling missing person cases.

Renee Bruhl was just 19 years old when she went missing from Indiana Dunes State Park in July 1966. She has hazel eyes and brown hair, and at the time of her disappearance, she was 5 feet 9 inches tall and weighed 135 pounds. She was last seen wearing a brown bathing suit with green flowers and gold leaves.

Patricia Blough was just 19 years old when she went missing from Indiana Dunes State Park in July 1966. She has brown eyes and brown hair, and at the time of her disappearance, she was 5 feet 4 inches tall and weighed 115 pounds. She was last seen wearing a yellow bikini with ruffles.

Ann Miller was just 21 years old when she went missing from Indiana Dunes State Park in July 1966. She has blue eyes and brown hair, and at the time of her disappearance, she was 5 feet 2 inches tall and weighed 110 pounds. She was last seen wearing a blue two-piece bathing suit with a red belt.

If you have any information about Renee, Patty, and Ann, please contact the Indiana State Police at 219-269-4747.

Joshua Guimond

Joshua Guimond, a junior at St. John's University in Collegeville, Minnesota, went to a party with a few of his friends on the evening of Saturday, November 9, 2002. It was a small gathering of less than 10 people, and it was held in a Metten Court dorm room. Josh left the room shortly before midnight, and his friends assumed he was going down the hall to use the bathroom. When he didn't return after 15 minutes, they wondered if he had decided to return to his on-campus apartment. They tried calling him there; when they got no answer, they thought he was already asleep. Josh wasn't asleep, though, and he never made it back to his apartment. He was never seen again.

Josh grew up in Maple Lake, Minnesota. He was a political science major at St. John's, and he was a popular student with a lot of friends. St. John's was a fairly small school, with about 1850 students. Located 75 miles northwest of Minneapolis, it provided a quiet and tranquil learning environment. Surrounded by acres of woods and a number of lakes, students would often joke that they were separated from the rest of society by a pine curtain. They viewed their campus as a utopian place and rarely thought about safety.

Josh planned on a future in politics after graduation. He was the treasurer of the pre-law society and the co-captain of the university's mock trial team. An honors student, he was considered responsible, logical, and very organized. He tutored other students and loved to spend hours debating political and legal issues. His grandmother had served two terms in the Minnesota House of Representatives, and Josh wanted to follow in her footsteps. He even used "Senator Josh" as his email name.

Josh spent the afternoon before the party working on a paper he was writing about Alexander Hamilton. He then relaxed with a couple of friends at his apartment for a few hours, drinking beer and talking about the future. Around 11:00 pm, the group decided to meet up with a few other friends, so they left Josh's St. Maur House apartment and walked the short distance across campus to Metten Court. There, they continued drinking beer and played a couple of card games. Friends saw Josh leave the room about 30 minutes after arriving and assumed he was just going off to use the restroom. No one reported seeing Josh leave Metten Court and no one would recall seeing him walking back to his apartment. His movements once he walked out of his friend's room are completely unknown.

Josh was scheduled to be at a mock trial meeting the next afternoon at 2:30 pm. When he didn't show up, several of his teammates tried to reach him at his apartment but got no answer. It was out of character for Josh to miss any meetings, so his friends immediately feared something was wrong. After comparing notes, they realized that no one had seen Josh since the night before. His car was still parked in his assigned parking spot, and nothing seemed to be missing from his apartment. Concerned, they alerted campus police that they believed Josh was missing.

The campus police were not initially worried. Although it was unlike Josh to disappear, he was a 20-year-old college student. They assumed he had simply met up with some other friends and taken off for the night. They conducted a cursory search of campus that night but found nothing to indicate where Josh might have gone.

Josh's friends and classmates hoped that he would show up the next day with a good story about where he had been. When he was absent from his classes on Monday morning, they knew something was wrong. They called the Stearns County Sheriff's Department and reported Josh missing. Deputies conducted a massive search for Josh that day, combing through the entire 2400 acres of St. John's campus as well as 700 adjacent acres of woodland.

Search dogs were brought in to see if they could track where Josh might have gone when he left Metten Court. In order to go back to his apartment in St. Maur House, Josh would have had to cross over Stumpf Lake using one of two bridges. After tracking dogs seemed to pick up his scent near a culvert at the east end of Stumpf Lake, deputies worried that Josh might have fallen into the lake. Although the waters were relatively calm, the water temperature was only a few degrees above freezing. If Josh had fallen in, he would not have been able to survive for long. An extensive search of the lake failed to produce any evidence that Josh was in the water, but police would continue to monitor the area.

A Minnesota State Patrol helicopter flew over the campus using infrared radar but found nothing relevant to the search. Deputies on horseback scoured the wooded areas surrounding the campus, and volunteers assisted in searching the campus. Police contacted all the hunters who had participated in a controlled deer hunt near campus on Sunday afternoon, but none of them had seen anything unusual in the woods.

Josh's parents arrived at the university on Monday afternoon, and they made tearful pleas for information about what had happened to their son. Brian Guimond would spend the next several nights sleeping in his son's apartment, speaking with students about Josh and gathering ideas for possible search areas. He participated in several news conferences and made a passionate plea for residents in the area to check their properties for clues to Josh's whereabouts. He was convinced Josh had been abducted.

Police found nothing to indicate any foul play had taken place, and they believed that Josh had most likely fallen into the lake and drowned. They pointed out that Josh had been drinking prior to his disappearance, and may have stumbled into the water and been too intoxicated to get out. His friends, however, noted that Josh had not seemed to be at all impaired that night. Although they admitted he had consumed about 10 beers, he had done so over the course of six hours and had appeared to be perfectly sober during the walk to Metten Court less than an hour before he went missing.

Members of the National Guard were sent to the campus on Wednesday, and they went through the entire area a second time to make sure nothing had been missed during the initial search. The university also allowed law enforcement access to all campus buildings, including dormitories, classrooms, and the abbey. Searching through the private living quarters of the priests who stayed in the abbey would normally have required a search warrant, but the school allowed deputies unhindered access to the location and cooperated fully in the investigation into Josh's disappearance. Nothing was found to indicate Josh was being held anywhere on campus.

Over the course of three days, an area of 20 square miles was thoroughly searched multiple times, but nothing was found. Police grew increasingly convinced that Josh would be found in one of the lakes on campus. They worked with university officials to lower the water level in Stumpf Lake; though the lake was fairly shallow, the water was very murky. Divers were sent in several times without success, so the lake was dragged once the water level had been lowered. Again, there was nothing found to indicate Josh was in Stumpf Lake. Divers were sent in again a week later, this time with side-scan sonar equipment that gave them a detailed look at the bottom of the lake. They found no evidence of Josh.

Detectives interviewed Josh's family, friends, and classmates, but found nothing to indicate he would have planned his own disappearance. He was known around campus for being responsible and level-headed, and he was doing well in all of his classes. A search of his computer turned up nothing; his search history was free of anything incriminating and he favored humor websites and political discussion groups. They found several articles he had downloaded the afternoon before he disappeared, and all of them pertained to his research paper on Alexander Hamilton.

While Josh's parents continued to believe that he had been abducted from campus, police were still leaning towards the theory that he had fallen into a lake and drowned. They noted that if he had ended up in the water, the weather was going to play a huge part in their effort to recover his body. If the air temperature stayed consistent, they believed he could float to the surface within a day or two. If temperatures started to drop, however, ice would start to form on the lake's surface and his body might remain trapped underwater until the spring thaw.

By the second week of the search, the lake had started to freeze over, but police continued to search around it, convinced they would find Josh there. Although very little was done over the Christmas break, deputies returned to campus on January 8th and a dive team was sent into Gemini Lake, adjacent to the area where Josh was last seen. On his walk from Metten Court to St. Maur House, Josh would have crossed a bridge near a culvert leading from Stumpf Lake to Gemini Lake. Since their extensive search of Stumpf Lake had yielded no sign of Josh, detectives believed it was possible he could have fallen and ended up in Gemini Lake. Unfortunately, this search was as unsuccessful as all the previous searches.

In April, the search for Josh was renewed. His father took time off from work and spent hours kayaking on the campus lakes, praying for answers. He still thought Josh had been abducted, but was keeping an open mind and knew there was a possibility the lake might finally give up its secrets. He carefully monitored the water temperature each day, but even the warmer water failed to produce any evidence of his son.

In May, the Trident Foundation arrived on campus to do their own search of the lakes. Known as the country's leading authority on water search and rescue, they were confident that they would be able to find Josh if he were indeed in the water. They spent days sending divers into the lakes, using specialized equipment to aid them in their search. One by one, they cleared all the bodies of water on campus, and they determined that Josh was not there. Their executive director told police that his recommendation was to take the search in a different direction; Josh had not fallen into one of the lakes.

For Josh's parents, the Trident search simply confirmed what they already knew: Josh was not on campus. Something must have happened to him that night that made it impossible for him to make it home. Detectives were at a loss. They had interviewed everyone who had been on campus the night Josh went missing, and no one had seen or heard anything unusual. They were confident Josh had not staged his own disappearance, and now the idea that he had drowned in one of the lakes seemed to be impossible as well. They were willing to consider the possibility of foul play but had no evidence pointing in any direction. The investigation stalled.

Students at St. John's no longer felt as safe as they once had on the isolated campus. There were whispers about what might have happened to Josh, and rumors ran rampant. One centered around the priests that lived in the abbey on campus. Several of them were known to drink heavily, and some students believed that one of them had been returning to campus at the time Josh was walking back to his apartment and had accidentally run him over, then hid the body to avoid being prosecuted for drunk driving. Although the rumor spread wildly, police found nothing to indicate that there had been any kind of hit and run; a crash violent enough to cause death usually leaves behind small traces of evidence. They had not found any blood or car pieces to indicate Josh had been hit.

Despite the efforts of family and friends to keep the investigation going, the case eventually went cold. Sporadic searches continued to be conducted whenever any new tips were called in, but nothing brought police closer to locating Josh. In 2011, Lamar Outdoor Adventures donated two billboards to the Guimond family, and they were placed along Stearns County highways to remind people that Josh was still missing. A few tips trickled in, but nothing that advanced the investigation.

There has never been any activity on Josh's credit cards and his bank account remains untouched. Detectives monitor his social security number, and it has never been used. His disappearance remains one of the great mysteries of Minnesota, but police believe there is someone out there who knows what happened to Josh and can provide the information needed to solve this case and give the Guimond family some long-awaited closure.

Joshua Guimond was just 20 years old when he went missing from Collegeville, Minnesota in November 2002. He has blond hair and blue eyes, and at the time of his disappearance, he was 5 feet 11 inches tall and weighed approximately 170 pounds. He has a 4-inch long scar on his shoulder, and normally wears glasses or contact lenses. He was last seen wearing a gray hooded sweatshirt and blue jeans. If you have any information about Josh, please call the Stearns County Sheriff's Department at 320-259-3700.

Cleashindra Hall

Cleashindra Hall was having the time of her life in May 1994. The 18-year-old had just attended her senior prom and was getting ready for her graduation from Watson Chapel High School in Pine Bluff, Arkansas. Cleashindra – known as Clea to family and friends – was a superstar at her high school. An honor roll student, she was graduating at the top of her class and scheduled to give a speech at commencement. After graduation, she was going to Boston to attend a leadership conference, then she would be starting an internship at a pediatrician's office. She saw it as the first step towards her ultimate goal – she wanted to be a doctor. She had received a scholarship to Tennessee State University and was scheduled to enter their pre-med program in the fall. Clea was on the road to adulthood, and she could hardly wait.

In order to save extra money for college, Clea had a part-time job working for Dr. Larry Amos. Amos wasn't a medical doctor; he ran a non-profit organization out of an office attached to his home. Clea, who lived only a few blocks away, did clerical work for him after school and on weekends.

Clea was scheduled to work at 5:00 pm on Monday, May 9, 1994. Although she lived close to the office, one of her parents always drove her to and from work. On this day, her mother, Laurell, dropped her off. Clea told Laurell she would give her a call when she was finished with her work for the evening, and the two said goodbye. Laurell watched as Clea disappeared into the office, unaware that it would be the last time she would see her daughter.

Around 8:00 pm, Clea called home and spoke to her mother. She wanted to know if anyone had called the house for her that evening, but no one had. She told her mom that she still had some work to do and would call back when she was ready to leave.

While she waited for Clea to call for a ride, Laurell dozed off on the couch. Clea never worked past 10:30 pm, and Laurell knew from experience that the ringing phone would wake her up from her nap. On this night, though, the phone never rang. Laurell woke up at 12:45 am when her husband, Willie, returned home from work. She was startled to see what time it was and immediately called Larry Amos at home to see if Clea was still working.

Larry answered his phone on the first ring. He told Laurell that Clea had signed out of work at 8:30 pm; he had seen her getting into a car but didn't know who the person was. Confused, Laurell thanked him and hung up the phone.

Laurell's first reaction was mild annoyance. She thought perhaps Clea was just acting out a little, a subtle reminder to her parents that she would soon be an independent adult living away from home. Yet Clea had never been the type to do anything like this, and Laurell had no idea who might have picked her up from work. Annoyance soon turned to concern as the hours went by with no sign of Clea. Laurell sat up and stared out her window for the rest of the night, sleepless with worry about her daughter.

Clea was supposed to be at school early on Tuesday for band practice. Although she had stayed out all night, no one thought she would skip school. Her younger brother looked for Clea as soon as he got to Watson

Chapel, but there was no sign of her. He immediately phoned his parents and told them that Clea was nowhere to be found. Panicked, Laurell called the Pine Bluff Police Department and attempted to report her daughter missing. Since Clea was legally an adult, police said they couldn't take a missing person report until she had been missing for at least 24 hours.

Willie and Laurell spent the day calling everyone they could think of that might know where Clea was, but no one had seen her. They waited impatiently until 5:00 pm, then drove to the Pine Bluff police station and filled out a missing person report. Police took the report – they were legally obligated to – but they didn't seem too concerned and did nothing to search for Clea. They told the Halls that Clea was likely out with friends and would return home soon.

Laurell knew in her heart that Clea would never go anywhere without calling her family. She wasn't the type of teenager who would run away from home, and she hadn't taken anything with her. Her purse, identification, and all her belongings were still in her bedroom. She didn't even have her own bank account yet. Refusing to wait for the police to act, the family decided to launch their own search for Clea. They decided to search the wooded lot across the street from the Amos house first. They scoured the area but found nothing of interest. The Halls weren't sure if they were relieved or disappointed; they wanted to find Clea, but they certainly didn't want to find her dead in the woods. They made flyers with her information and started posting them all over town, but received no leads.

After Clea had been missing for a few days, detectives finally got involved in the search. They began interviewing those people closest to Clea, and were particularly interested in a male student some believed was Clea's boyfriend. The student was asked to submit to a polygraph examination, and he agreed; the results were inconclusive. He gave police permission to search his vehicle, and they were unable to find anything connecting him to Clea.

Police spoke with Larry Amos and several other employees who had seen Clea on the night she went missing. Larry told police the same thing he told Clea's parents: he had seen her getting into an unknown vehicle around 8:30 pm. Another employee, however, told a slightly different story. She signed out of work around 8:25 pm and offered Clea a ride home. Clea declined, and told her coworker that she was going to walk home – something she had never done before. It's highly unlikely Clea would have attempted to walk home, so it's unclear why she told her coworker this. She may have been trying to hide the identity of the person picking her up, or the coworker may have misunderstood her.

Police didn't do an initial search of Larry's office until Clea had already been missing for two weeks. They found nothing suspicious; there were no signs of a fight and no evidence anyone had been injured there. Clea's parents were highly critical of the amount of time that passed before the search was completed, noting that if anything had happened in the office there had been ample time to get rid of any evidence. Police stated that there had been multiple people present in the office when Clea left and they had no reason to believe anything had happened to her there that night.

Although they had been slow to start the investigation, police quickly realized that Clea had likely been the victim of foul play. They agreed with her parents that there was no reason for her to leave voluntarily; she had a bright future ahead of her and no reason to want to abandon her life. She also wasn't the type who would get in a car with anyone she didn't know. Detectives believe that she was picked up by someone familiar to her, and that person is responsible for her disappearance. Despite following a number of leads, however, they have never been able to establish the type of vehicle that picked Clea up nor the identity of the driver.

Clea's parents were very suspicious of Larry Amos from the start. As far as they were concerned, he was the last person to see their daughter, making him a logical suspect. The day after Clea went missing, he left on a business trip to Texas and wasn't available to be interviewed by police until nearly two weeks after the disappearance. He also refused to take a polygraph examination. With no physical evidence linking him to any crime, however, there was little police could do.

Detectives told the news media that they had several persons of interest in Clea's disappearance, but never named any suspects. Although leads continued to trickle in, the case quickly went cold. Clea's family refused to let the case be forgotten. Pink bows were placed all over town – including on police cars – to remind people that Clea was still missing. Every year, the family held a balloon release on Clea's birthday and continued to pray for information about what happened that May night.

In 2012, it looked as if their prayers might finally be answered. A construction worker who had done some work for Larry Amos in the late 1990s went to police and told them he had seen what he believed to be blood splattered on some of the insulation in Larry's home. Another worker noted that he had smelled an extremely foul odor while doing some work on the property around the same time. It's unclear why these men waited nearly 20 years before coming forward, but with the information they provided police were able to obtain a search warrant for the property.

Investigators descended on the Amos home on March 29, 2012. Cadaver dogs and radar equipment were used to search the home, office, and surrounding property. While police saw no overt signs of blood, they removed four bags of evidence from the home to be submitted for further testing. Larry Amos had no comment for the swarms of news cameras that set up camp outside his home, but police said he did cooperate with the search.

Willie and Laurell were hopeful that they would finally learn what happened to their daughter, but the case took a bizarre turn. Instead of passing the bags of evidence to crime scene technicians, a detective put the items in the trunk of his car. He said he did so because he was parked in the driveway of the house while the crime scene investigations truck had parked a block away; with all the media personnel flooding the area he thought it would be the quickest way to get the evidence out of the home. Unfortunately, rather than return to the police station and log the items into evidence, the detective drove home for the night, leaving the items to sit in his trunk until the next day. This left some questions about the chain of custody and integrity of the evidence.

The police chief assured the Hall family that the items had been sent to the lab to check for the presence of blood, and they would know shortly what the results were. Willie and Laurell waited, as days and then weeks went by without any answers. A month later, when they spoke with police chief Brenda Davis-Jones, the chief assured them that the items were in the process of being tested. She said any delay was caused by the Arkansas State Crime Lab, not police. Unfortunately, the Halls soon learned this was a lie – the police had never even sent the evidence to the lab.

Clea's friends and family were outraged at the delay. They accused the department of being incompetent and hindering the investigation. The evidence was finally sent out, but test results showed no blood on any of the items collected from the Amos house. The Halls, however, weren't convinced and wondered if there was some kind of police conspiracy to keep the identity of the killer unknown. Police denied all accusations.

After the search of the Amos property, the case once again went cold. Clea's family is still looking for her, and will not rest until they know what happened to her that night.

Cleashindra Hall was just 18 years old when she went missing from Pine Bluff, Arkansas in May 1994. She has brown eyes and black hair, and at the time of her disappearance, she was 5 feet 8 inches tall and weighed 120 pounds. She had a chipped front tooth and a surgical scar on her left knee. When last seen, she was wearing a navy blue and white two-piece shorts set that had polka dots on the shorts and stripes on the shirt, white socks, and white sneakers. She was wearing small stud earrings, press-on nails, hair extensions, and a white bow in her hair. If you have any information about Cleashindra, please call the Pine Bluff Police Department at 870-543-5111.

Kelly Hollan

Kelly Hollan had an unexpected day off from kindergarten on February 12, 1982. Knotts County, Kentucky had been hit with a heavy snowstorm and school had been canceled as a result. After he ate breakfast, he begged his mother, Judy Moore, to be allowed to go out and play in the snow. Judy initially told him no; Kelly had asthma and she didn't think it was a good idea for him to go out in such cold weather. Eventually, she gave in to his pleas and helped him put on snow boots and his heavy winter coat. After cautioning him not to leave the yard, she sent him outside at 11:00 am.

Judy had been a very young mother. She dropped out of school when she was just 14 years old and married Bobby Hollan. By 1974, the couple had two children, Robert and Margaret. A third child had been born premature and only survived a few weeks. Neither Bobby nor Judy had a job; Judy said she had epilepsy that prevented her from working. The state of Kentucky removed Robert and Margaret from the home, ruling that Judy wasn't taking adequate care of them. Her parents stepped in and took custody of both children, but it wasn't long before Judy got pregnant again. Kelly was born in November 1975; the state of Kentucky doesn't appear to have raised any questions about Judy's ability to parent him and she retained custody of Kelly. She and Bobby soon divorced, and she told people that Kelly was all she had.

Judy and Kelly moved in with her boyfriend in Pine Tree Hollow in 1981. It was an extremely rural area, with gravel roads and just a few houses scattered around the hollow. Due to its remoteness, Judy felt it was quite safe to allow 6-year-old Kelly to play outside unsupervised. She checked on him through the window a few times that afternoon, and he seemed to be having fun entertaining himself in the snow.

Judy went to a neighbor's home at 4:00 pm to use their phone. She and her boyfriend didn't have a phone of their own, and she needed to talk to her sister. Kelly was still playing outside at the time. After chatting with her sister, she returned home. Kelly was no longer in the yard, but she assumed he went to visit a friend down the street. The two boys would often watch television together – Kelly loved the Dukes of Hazzard – so Judy figured Kelly would return home once the show was over.

Judy made dinner around 6:00 pm and went outside to see if she could find Kelly, but he still hadn't returned. She decided to eat without him. After she finished her meal, she walked to the home of Kelly's friend and asked if Kelly was there. She was surprised to learn that Kelly hadn't been there at all that day.

Judy claimed that once she learned Kelly was missing, she went to the home of her boyfriend's grandparents so she could use their phone to call police. For some reason, she said they refused to allow her to use the phone until midnight. It's unclear why she didn't attempt to go somewhere else to use a phone; by the time she called to report the child missing, he had been gone for at least six hours and possibly more.

The Knott County Rescue Squad was dispatched immediately and began searching the area for the missing child. They initially assumed that he had simply wandered off and gotten lost and expected to find him quickly. At 1:51 am, the rescue squad called the Kentucky State Police and alerted them that the situation appeared to be more serious as they had found no sign of Kelly. The first state trooper arrived on the scene at 3:00 am.

The earliest hours of the search were hampered by a lack of manpower on the overnight shift as well as by the fact that it had started to snow again. By daylight, however, dozens of officials were involved in the search for Kelly. Most assumed the boy was lost or injured; the area was so remote that abduction didn't seem likely. Their main concern was that Kelly might have tumbled into one of the abandoned mineshafts that dotted the area. New snowfall had eradicated any footprints the boy might have left, so they used search dogs to try and pick up his scent. The dogs seemed unable to pick up a scent trail.

Judy called her parents to tell them that Kelly was missing. Their reaction was likely not what she expected; they seemed to think Judy had done something to her son. Judy's father lamented the fact that he and his wife only had custody of Margaret and Robert, saying that if they had custody of Kelly he wouldn't have disappeared.

Initial reports indicated that a friend of Kelly's had seen him on the afternoon he disappeared; the boy stated that he and Kelly had walked to a small store located in the hollow around 4:00 pm. Later reports omitted this supposed sighting, it's unclear if police were able to rule it out or if the child reporting it had his days mixed up. No one else reported seeing Kelly at all that day.

Judy believed that Kelly's father likely had something to do with the abduction, but police were able to verify that he had been nowhere near Pine Tree Hollow on the day he went missing. Judy's sister claimed that Judy had killed Kelly and asked her for help hiding his body, but Judy denied this and her sister later retracted her statement.

The search for Kelly continued for more than two weeks. Police combed through Pine Tree Hollow looking for any evidence that might lead to the missing child, but found nothing. They drained wells and dragged creeks, searched through abandoned mines, dug up several different areas, and checked under homes and porches.

One neighbor thought she recalled seeing a green car in the area on the day Kelly went missing but without any other information police were unable to determine if this car had anything to do with the disappearance.

Police looked into rumors that Judy was somehow responsible for whatever happened to Kelly, but were unable to find any evidence to substantiate these claims. Several of the detectives believed Judy was involved, but also noted that several of the people living in the area had criminal records and none could be ruled out. A grand jury investigation took place, but no one was ever indicted in the case. The investigation soon went cold.

Sporadic searches for Kelly continued to take place over the years. In 2008, detectives received a tip that Kelly had been killed and buried under the concrete porch of his former home. Investigators dug around the entire foundation of the porch but found nothing. The case remains open, and detectives continue to follow up on new leads as they learn of them. They do not believe Kelly was abducted; they believe he was likely murdered on the same day he was reported missing and are hoping to one day get the information they need to close the case.

In 2021, Judy told reporters that detectives seemed intent on getting her to confess to harming her son but said she had nothing to do with his disappearance. At one point, she said investigators told her that her sister confessed to helping her dispose of Kelly's body. She was stunned and told them that she believed her son was still alive somewhere. Even decades after she last saw her little boy, she still hoped to be reunited with him.

Kelly Junior Hollan was just 6 years old when he went missing from Hindman, Kentucky in February 1982. He has brown hair and blue eyes, and at the time of his disappearance, he was 4 feet tall and weighed 60 pounds. He was born with a cleft palate and has a scar on the left side of his face between his upper lip and his nose, and he had a noticeable speech impediment. He was last seen wearing a blue winter coat with a hood and snow boots. If you have any information on Kelly, please contact the Kentucky State Police at 606-435-6069.

Kyron Horman

Kyron Horman was excited about going to school on June 4, 2010. The 7-year-old was participating in his school's science fair that day, and he had spent weeks perfecting his project on the red-eyed tree frog. Kyron's stepmother, Terri Horman, drove him to Skyline Elementary School in Portland, Oregon and helped him get set up at the science fair. Once everything looked perfect, Terri snapped a quick picture of Kyron, smiling proudly as he displayed his project. Terri caught a final glimpse of Kyron as she left the school at 8:45 am; he was walking down the hallway towards his second-grade classroom.

Kyron was born to Kaine Horman and Desiree Young, who divorced while Desiree was still pregnant with Kyron. They shared joint custody of their son until 2004, when Desiree was diagnosed with kidney failure and Kaine was granted full custody. Kaine married Terri in 2007, and they had a daughter together in 2008. Kyron lived with them in Portland, Oregon, and attended school just two miles away from his home. Desiree, who also remarried, lived six hours away in Medford, Oregon, but remained an important part of Kyron's life. Kyron had wanted her to see his science fair project, but Desiree had been unable to take time off from work. Kyron was going to be spending the weekend in Medford with her and her husband, though, and planned to tell her all about red-eyed tree frogs when he got there.

Kaine Horman, who worked for Intel, returned home from work that day at 2:00 pm. Terri and their daughter, Kiara, were at the house when he got there. At 3:35 pm, the three of them walked down to Kyron's bus stop to meet him after school. Kaine was looking forward to hearing about the science fair; he had been very proud of the amount of time and effort Kyron had put into his project.

The school bus arrived around 3:45 pm as usual, but Kyron wasn't on it. Kaine wondered if Kyron had been confused by the fact that Terri had driven him to school that morning. Perhaps he had expected her to pick him up at the school that afternoon. Terri quickly called the school to see if he was still there but was told that Kyron hadn't been in class that day. None of the staff at the school recalled seeing him at all. His teacher remembered having a conversation with Terri the previous week about Kyron having a doctor's appointment and believed that was why the child was absent. Assuming it was an excused absence, the school hadn't called the Hormans at home.

Kaine and Terri were momentarily paralyzed with fear. Kyron did have a doctor's appointment scheduled for the following Friday, but he had been dropped off at the school that morning and should have been in class. Fearing the child had been abducted, Kaine called police and reported Kyron missing. Police immediately began searching the area surrounding Skyline Elementary School, hoping the little boy had simply wandered off school property. The school, located in a hilly area to the west of downtown Portland, was surrounded by dense brush and steep inclines. It wasn't an easy area to search, and a drenching rainstorm that afternoon further complicated things.

Hours passed, and searchers found nothing to indicate what might have happened to Kyron. The Multnomah County Sheriff's Office wasn't sure if they were dealing with an abduction or a lost child, but didn't want to take any chances. They called the FBI, and the agency immediately dispatched its Child Abduction Rapid Deployment team to assist in the search. A large-scale physical search took place on Saturday, with police and volunteers continuing to scour the dense brush around Kyron's school.

On Sunday, detectives started their investigation with the Skyline Elementary School community. More than 200 children and their parents were interviewed about the day Kyron went missing, but no new information was learned.

Kyron's disappearance was front-page news across the Pacific Northwest. As word spread about the missing child, tips started flooding in. More than 1200 tips were phoned in during the first 72 hours of the search; most came from the Portland area, but possible sightings were reported across the entire state of Oregon and parts of Washington.

On Monday, investigators set up a checkpoint on the road near Kyron's school, and they stopped each car that drove into the area. They handed out flyers with Kyron's information and asked drivers if they had seen anything unusual the previous Friday. Everyone wanted to help in the investigation, but no one recalled seeing anything useful.

Hundreds of additional search and rescue experts from across the state came to assist in the search for Kyron. Although police appreciated the help offered by volunteer searchers, the terrain made searching dangerous and at least one searcher had to be taken away by ambulance after being injured in a fall. Residents were asked to check their own properties and sheds while professional search teams continued searching the area between Kyron's home and school.

A week after Kyron went missing, his parents and stepparents united to speak at a press conference. They thanked the searchers for all their hard work and pleaded with anyone who had any information to call police. Desiree noted that her son was timid about new situations and rarely strayed from his own front yard. He was not the sort of child that would go off on outdoor adventures; he was practically blind without his glasses and was severely allergic to bees.

Kaine and Desiree had been adamant from the start that Kyron wouldn't run away or wander off, and they were certain that he had been abducted. Ten days after the little boy went missing, police seemed to confirm this; the missing person investigation was officially reclassified as a criminal investigation. Detectives wouldn't give any reason for the status change and said they had no suspects or persons of interest. They did, however, comment that Kyron's disappearance seemed to be an isolated case; parents were told there was no reason for them to take any extra precautions with their own children.

Those following the case closely were shocked when, 24 days after Kyron went missing, Kaine Horman filed for divorce. He also requested and was granted a restraining order against Terri. She was prohibited from any contact with Kaine, their daughter, or her teenage son from a previous marriage. The Multnomah County Sheriff's Office refused to comment on any personal issues between Kaine and Terri, but once again stated that Terri was not considered a suspect in Kyron's disappearance. Kaine, Desiree, and Desiree's husband continued to work together in the search for Kyron but indicated that Terri had expressed little interest in the investigation since the very beginning.

Terri was never named a suspect in Kyron's case, but court documents filed by Kaine in the divorce case would paint a very different picture of her. He indicated that he believed Terri was responsible for Kyron's disappearance and she posed a significant safety threat to their daughter. Additionally, he had learned from investigators that, in late 2009, Terri had attempted to hire a landscaper to kill her husband. It was learning about this murder-for-hire plot that pushed Kaine over the edge. Prior to this, he believed his relationship with Terri was a good one and had not suspected her of any wrongdoing.

Kaine and Desiree held a press conference shortly after the public learned of the murder-for-hire scheme. Desiree admitted that she had suspected Terri immediately, but both she and Kaine believed Kyron was still alive somewhere. The public seemed less optimistic, particularly when Kaine noted that Terri had taken two polygraph examinations and failed them both. Police refused to comment on the issue.

Desiree made a very public plea for Terri to come forward and tell the truth about what happened to Kyron. She told reporters that Terri was not cooperating with the investigation; she had hired a lawyer and refused to speak with detectives.

As the investigation moved into its fourth week, it became apparent that detectives were taking a closer look at Terri Horman. They also believed there had been another adult with her when she drove Kyron to school for the science fair. Police designed a flyer with pictures of Terri, her white pickup truck, and her friend Dede Spicher. All residents who lived within a 4-mile radius of Skyline Elementary School were sent a copy of the flyer along with a questionnaire asking if they recalled seeing the women or the truck in the area between 8:45 am and 1:00 pm on the day Kyron went missing.

Several witnesses reported to investigators that they had seen Kyron walking across the parking lot with Terri on the day he went missing, and they believed there was another adult waiting in Terri's truck at that time. Terri has always denied this, and Dede told police she was at work the day Kyron went missing. Dede would later pass a polygraph and has always maintained that she had absolutely nothing to do with the disappearance.

Many people seemed convinced that Terri had done something to Kyron, but detectives were unable to find any physical evidence to support this theory. Not wanting to be accused of tunnel vision, investigators continued pursuing other possibilities. They interviewed all the registered sex offenders in the area. They pulled visitor logs from Skyline Elementary School for the week Kyron went missing and combed through them. They followed up on every possible sighting of the child that was reported. They even obtained phone logs and followed up with people who had made cell phone calls that were routed from the tower closest to the elementary school on the morning Kyron disappeared. In the first year of the investigation, the task force interviewed more than 3500 people and spent more than 26,000 hours working on the case. Nothing brought them any closer to finding Kyron.

In June 2012, Desiree filed a civil lawsuit against Terri Horman. In addition to asking for monetary damages, she asked a judge to order Kyron's former stepmother to either return him or lead authorities to his remains. Terri filed a motion to delay the lawsuit as it was seeking information that could result in criminal prosecution. Although a judge initially ruled that there was no reason to delay, Desiree eventually dropped the lawsuit. Terri still maintains she had nothing to do with Kyron's disappearance and she has no idea where he is.

Kaine and Terri's divorce was finalized in 2013 and Kaine was granted full custody of Kiara. In June 2014, Terri went to court asking to change her name from Terri Lynn Moulton Horman to Claire Stella Sullivan. She claimed that her name had been stigmatized due to the investigation and it was impossible for her to find a job. She wanted to make a fresh start with a new name, but the judge rejected the request. She was eventually able to find a job as a mental health support specialist but left after just two months because she claimed she was being harassed and stalked. She tried to get a restraining order against the woman she said was stalking her, but a judge found no basis for her claim and denied the request.

There have been numerous searches for Kyron in the decade since he went missing, but no evidence of the little boy has ever been found. While Desiree and Kaine tried to remain optimistic, they have come to terms with the fact that Kyron is most likely deceased. No charges have ever been filed in his case.

Kyron Horman was just 7 years old when he went missing from Portland, Oregon in June 2010. He has brown hair and blue eyes, and at the time of his disappearance, he was 3 feet 8 inches tall and weighed 50 pounds. He was last seen wearing a black CSI t-shirt with green lettering and the image of a handprint on the front, black cargo pants, white athletic socks, and black Skechers sneakers with orange trim. He was also wearing metal-framed eyeglasses. If you have any information about Kyron, please contact the Multnomah County Sheriff's Office at 503-823-3333.

Sofia Juarez

Sofia Juarez was in an excited mood on the evening of February 4, 2003. Her fifth birthday was the next day, and she was looking forward to opening her presents. She spent most of the night in her room playing with her Barbie dolls but came out around 8:00 pm when she overheard her grandmother's boyfriend, Jose Torres, say he had to run to a nearby convenience store. Sofia loved going places, so she asked her mother, Maria, if she could tag along with Jose. Maria agreed that she could go, and gave her a dollar so she could buy herself a treat. She helped Sofia tie her white Converse sneakers, gave her a hug, and told her to have fun. Sofia skipped happily out the door, clutching her dollar bill. It was the last time Maria would see her daughter.

Maria and Sofia had moved in with Maria's mother, Ignacia, two years before. Ignacia's home on East 15th Street in Kennewick, Washington was crowded – six of Maria's siblings as well as Jose Torres also lived there – but they were a close family and Sofia loved being surrounded by so many relatives. Sofia often seemed shy and reserved around people she didn't know well, but she was bubbly and fun-loving around her family. She had no contact with her biological father but considered Jose to be part of her family and enjoyed going to places with him.

Jose was usually more than happy to have the little girl tag along with him, but on this particular evening, he was unaware that Sofia had been planning to come with him and left without her. By the time Sofia came outside, his car had already pulled out of the driveway. It's not entirely clear what happened next, but police believe Sofia decided she was going to walk the five blocks to the store and meet Jose there. She never made it to the store, and she was never seen again.

Maria had no idea Jose left without taking Sofia; it wasn't until he returned home about 45 minutes later that she realized there was a problem. As soon as she learned Sofia wasn't with him, she gathered up the family and they began searching the neighborhood for the little girl. After 15 minutes of fruitless searching, Maria called the police.

Kennewick Police took the situation seriously from the start. The temperature had dropped below freezing, and Sofia had been wearing only a long-sleeved shirt and overalls. She had expected just to go on a short car ride so hadn't bothered to wear a coat. If she had gotten lost somewhere in the neighborhood, police knew they had to find her quickly. Police, with the help of volunteers, immediately launched a search for Sofia, going door-to-door to all the houses she would have passed on her walk to the store. Police checked underneath porches, in parked cars and trash cans, and down every side street.

When a 10-year-old neighbor told police he saw Sofia walk down her driveway and speak to a man wearing all black, police worried that someone had abducted the child. The Washington Office of Emergency Management issued its first statewide Amber Alert for Sofia, and Maria made a public plea for the return of her daughter. The FBI was called in to join the investigation, and agents arrived to help in the search.

By morning, there was still no sign of Sofia. The family spent the little girl's birthday assisting in the search for her and praying she would be found. Hundreds of police officers, firefighters, and volunteers walked shoulder-to-shoulder through fields and rural farmland, hoping for any clue to Sofia's whereabouts. Divers were sent into the Columbia River, located less than two miles from the Juarez home. An Army National Guard helicopter flew over vast areas using thermal imaging equipment, and search dogs were used to try to pick up Sofia's scent. They found nothing to indicate Sofia was still in the area.

Detectives continued to canvass the neighborhood looking for anyone who saw anything suspicious. They impounded Jose's car and asked him to come to the station for questioning. He voluntarily submitted to a polygraph examination; he passed and was eliminated as a suspect. Investigators tracked down Andres Abragan, Sofia's dad, and questioned him. He told police he had never met Sofia and wasn't even sure if he was actually her father, but agreed to take a polygraph. He also passed and was not considered a suspect. One by one, detectives were able to rule out all members of Sofia's immediate family from having anything to do with her disappearance.

A couple of people mentioned seeing a white van in the area on the night Sofia went missing, leading police to question a registered sex offender who lived in the area and had access to a similar van. Police impounded the van and searched the man's home without finding anything relevant to the investigation. The man was questioned extensively, but was eventually ruled out when he passed a polygraph and police could find nothing to suggest he had ever met Sofia.

By the end of the first week, police had received more than 200 tips about the case and had thoroughly investigated each one. All were dead ends. Every officer on the Kennewick Police force was assigned to the case in the hopes that they would be able to dig up some new leads but they found nothing. Despite the intensive search for the child, the news media paid relatively little attention to the case, and the number of tips coming in started to dwindle.

Maria didn't believe Sofia would have gone anywhere with someone she didn't know, leading detectives to explore the possibility that one of her relatives had abducted her and taken her to Mexico. It was a persistent rumor in the case, and Maria and Ignacia decided it was something they needed to investigate further. In March, they flew to Guadalajara and then traveled to Puebla, where they had family. They spent days tracking down people in Mexico but came back to the United States confident that Sofia had not been taken there.

The Columbia Basin Dive Rescue team was sent back to the river, where they expanded their search area to include three miles of water and shoreline. They left confident that Sofia was not going to be found in the water, though they would periodically search along the coastline just to be sure.

Detectives desperately wanted to find Sofia, but after exhausting all leads they admitted that they still had no suspects in the disappearance. The case slowly went cold, and those outside of the immediate neighborhood appeared to forget all about the missing child. Her case was never picked up by the national news media; many speculated this was because Sofia came from a poor family and was being raised by a single mother. Whatever the reason, the case languished in the cold case files for two years.

By 2005, police had interviewed more than 1200 people, administered two dozen polygraph examinations, and searched several houses and vehicles looking for evidence related to Sofia. After getting a tip from a confidential informant, a search was conducted on farmland near Prosser in King County. According to the informant, who was being held on drug charges and likely hoped to strike a deal with police, Sofia had been accidentally run over and her body had been buried behind some homes on the property. Police spent a week using cadaver dogs and then backhoes in several locations on the farm, but were unable to find anything to substantiate the tip.

Maria moved back to California in 2007, though she continued to call the Kennewick Police Department looking for updates on her daughter's case. She got married and was the mother of a 6-month-old son in 2009 when she died after experiencing complications from a medical procedure. She was only 26 years old and had always believed that Sofia was still alive somewhere. Her funeral mass was held in Kennewick, and a processional escorted Maria's ashes to the church from the corner of 15th Avenue and Washington Street, where her daughter had last been seen. It was a touching tribute and a way for the family to let everyone know that, despite losing Maria, they were going to continue the search for Sofia.

The Kennewick Police Department has never forgotten about Sofia, and there is always at least one detective assigned to work on her case. By 2020, the case file contained over 20,000 pages of information. In an attempt to get the case back out in the public eye, Kennewick Police and Washington State Police teamed up with a transportation company in February 2021; Sofia's picture and case information will be displayed on the sides of two trucks. Like a traveling billboard, the trucks also list the number to call with tips about the case. Sofia's family, noting that Sofia should have been celebrating her 23rd birthday in 2021, were pleased that the case was going to get some exposure and remain hopeful that they will one day learn what happened to her.

Sofia Lucerno Juarez was just 4 years old when she went missing from Kennewick, Washington in February 2003. She has black hair and brown eyes, and at the time she went missing she was 3 feet tall and weighed 30 pounds, and she was missing her four front top teeth. She has a mole under one eye and her ears are pierced; she normally wore gold hoop earrings. She was last seen wearing a red long-sleeved shirt, blue overalls, violet socks, and white Converse sneakers. If you have any information about Sofia, please contact the Kennewick Police Department at 509-585-4208.

Steven Koecher

Steven Koecher had high hopes for his future when he moved to St. George, Utah in the spring of 2009. By December, however, the 30-year-old was struggling to make ends meet. He was unable to find a full-time job and his bank account was nearly empty. Despite numerous setbacks, he maintained a positive attitude, leading his family to believe that everything was going to work out for him. Then, on December 13, 2009, he vanished.

Steven was born in Amarillo, Texas. He was the second oldest of five children and was raised in the Mormon church. He graduated from the University of Utah in 2002 with a degree in communications and worked for a while as a journalist at the Davis County Clipper, where his father was the executive editor. In 2007, he got a job at the Salt Lake Tribune. Although he liked the job, he wasn't thrilled about working the third shift hours it required. In 2009, he decided to quit his job and relocate somewhere a little warmer.

Steven moved to St. George in April and found a job in advertising. He was quickly accepted into the church community there and made a lot of friends through his local LDS singles ward. He became a mentor for the Big Brothers/Big Sisters program and coached several different youth sports. He remained close to his family and visited with them in Bountiful often.

Unfortunately, Steven was laid off from his job shortly after he moved to St. George and had a hard time finding a new one. The country was in the midst of the worst recession since the Great Depression, and there were far more people looking for work than there were available jobs. To try and keep himself afloat, Steven took a part-time job handing out advertisements for a window cleaning business. He wasn't earning enough to pay all his bills, though, and he quickly ran through any savings he had.

Steven's grandmother was aware of his tenuous financial situation and sent him a check in October. He never cashed it. He was adamant that he would find a way to make it on his own. His parents pleaded with him to return to Salt Lake City where he would be close to family, but Steven declined.

When Steven signed the lease on the room he was renting, he used his father, Rolf Koecher, as a reference. The first week in December, Steven's landlord called Rolf and told him that Steven was three months behind in his rent and had not returned any of his calls. Rolf had no idea things had gotten so bad, and he called Steven on December 9th to offer him financial help. Steven got upset with his father and hung up on him, but texted him the next day to apologize. He told his father he was okay and that he wanted to handle things on his own. He spoke with his mother the same day and told her that he would be returning home for Christmas and they could expect to see him on December 23rd. He seemed upbeat and excited about the upcoming holiday. He told his mother that he also planned to attend their annual family reunion on December 26th and would head back to St. George after that.

On December 17th, Rolf and Deanne Koecher received a phone call from a Henderson, Nevada Parking Enforcement officer. Steven's car had been parked on a street in a Henderson retirement community since

December 13th and was now considered abandoned. The officer had been trying to contact Steven for two days without success and was hoping his parents might know where he was. Rolf and Deanne Koecher were shocked. Henderson, located to the southeast of Las Vegas, was about 150 miles from Steven's home in St. George. No one had any idea why Steven would be in that area. The devout Mormon didn't drink or gamble, making Vegas seem like an unlikely destination for him.

All calls to Steven's cell phone went straight to voicemail. Deanne called the phone company to see if they could determine the location of the phone, but it was either switched off or disabled and could not be located. Certain that something was terribly wrong, Rolf and two of Steven's brothers immediately started driving to St. George to check Steven's apartment. When they arrived, Rolf used his spare key and opened the door slowly, unsure of what they would find inside. Everything seemed normal. It appeared that almost all of Steven's belongings were there, including his laptop and his cell phone charger. The kitchen was well-stocked with food. There was nothing to indicate that Steven had left under duress; everything appeared neat and orderly.

Rolf found the spare set of keys to Steven's car and the group drove to Henderson, where they soon located Steven's car. It had been parked on a quiet cul-de-sac in Sun City Anthem, an upscale 55+ community. This wasn't a place a lost tourist would simply stumble across; it wasn't directly connected to any major road and getting there involved making several different turns within the subdivision.

Inside the car, there were pillows and a blanket, indicating that Steven had likely slept in the car at some point. Coats, snacks, a shaving kit, and a bag containing what appeared to be Christmas gifts for Steven's niece and nephew were also found. The trunk of the car contained numerous copies of Steven's resume, and he had a stack of flyers from his part-time job sitting on the dashboard. The only things that appeared to be missing were Steven's car keys, wallet, and cell phone.

Rolf didn't see anything in the car that made him believe foul play had taken place, but he didn't find any indication of what Steven might have been doing in Henderson, either. The car started right up and its gas tank was half full. If Steven had abandoned his car, he hadn't done so due to any mechanical problems.

Unsure what to do, Rolf called the Henderson Police Department. The responding officers looked the car over but saw no reason to conduct a forensic examination of the vehicle or its contents. They assured Rolf that people regularly came to Las Vegas to disappear for a while, and they were sure Steven would turn up in a few days. Although Rolf was certain this was not the case, he didn't push the officers. The family would begin the search for Steven on their own.

Rolf and Steven's brothers started their search by canvassing the street where Steven's car had been found. They knocked on doors, asking if any of the residents had interacted with Steven or had noticed anything unusual. No one had. One man, however, told Rolf he had several security cameras on his property, and at least one of them covered the area where the car was found. He was happy to share it with them.

It took a couple of weeks for the footage to be downloaded, analyzed, and made available to the Koechers, but it was worth the wait. The surveillance footage showed Steven's car drive past the camera at 11:54 am on Sunday, December 13th. The spot where the car parked was just out of view of the camera, but at 12:00 pm a man could be seen walking from the direction where the car was parked. He appeared to be holding something, perhaps a folder, in one hand. As he walked down the sidewalk in front of the house, he was picked up by two different security cameras. He crossed the street onto Evening Lights Road and then continued down the sidewalk until he faded from view.

The Koechers were elated; the man was clearly Steven. He was walking rather quickly and appeared to know where he was going, and he didn't seem to be under duress. They still had no idea why he was in Henderson, but they were now certain he had been the last person to drive his car and wasn't a victim of a carjacking. Unfortunately, the trail ended here. Steven did not reappear on the surveillance footage.

The family examined Steven's phone records and financial statements as they tried to reconstruct what he had been doing in the days before he disappeared. They were surprised to learn that Steven had done a lot of traveling in the 72 hours before he went to Henderson. On December 10th, Steven had driven to Ruby Valley, Nevada – over 6 hours away from his home in St. George. While there, he stopped to visit with the parents of a girl he had briefly dated. They were surprised to see him as he showed up unannounced but invited him to have lunch with them. He told them that he was planning to travel to Sacramento. He left shortly after lunch but he didn't go towards Sacramento. Instead, he headed west. He stopped for gas in Springville, Utah, and then stopped for dinner at Taco Time in Nephi, Utah before finally heading home to St. George. During the time he was on the road, Steven spoke on the phone with his mother but didn't say anything about his travels.

On the morning of December 12th, Steven's cell phone records place him near Overton, Nevada, about 80 miles from his home. It's unclear what he was doing. He purchased gas in Mesquite, Nevada late that afternoon, then presumably made the 40-mile drive from there to St. George. He purchased a few Christmas gifts at the Kmart in his hometown later that evening. Neighbors saw him return to his home around 10:30 pm that night, but he only remained there for 30 minutes before he left again. No one knows where he spent the night; he was in the Las Vegas area the following morning.

Steven spoke to two different church members on Sunday, December 13th. The president of his ward called him around 9:00 am to see if he could possibly lead the 11:00 am meeting that morning. Steven said he was in Las Vegas but could return to St. George if necessary. The president told him not to worry about it. Steven was supposed to officiate the 1:00 pm service that day, and he didn't say anything about not being back in time. Interestingly, his phone records seem to indicate he was actually much further south than Las Vegas at this time.

Another church member called Steven around 11:00 am with an item he needed added to the 1:00 pm announcements. Steven told him that he wouldn't be there for the service. This was a surprise to church members, who noted that Steven had always let someone know well in advance if he wasn't going to be able to attend a meeting. This phone call was the last confirmed contact with Steven, but not the last time the phone was used. On the morning of December 14th, the day after Steven was last seen on surveillance video, his phone was used to call his voicemail. According to the family, the phone was still in the Las Vegas metro area at the time. No one knows if this call was made by Steven or someone else.

Sensing that the police weren't taking Steven's disappearance seriously, the family hired a private investigator. They also arranged for a local dairy to put Steven's information on half-gallon milk cartons to increase awareness about the case. It was a wise move; the increase in public interest led to the Henderson Police Department finally assigning detectives to investigate Steven's disappearance.

Police canvassed the development where the car had been found, but learned nothing new. Concerned that Steven might have ended up in the desert, police conducted a large-scale search on December 30th. Three different police departments took part, using ATVs, search dogs, and helicopters to comb through the rugged desert terrain that surrounded the Henderson area. Volunteers went door-to-door, speaking with residents and handing out flyers with Steven's information. Detectives contacted bus stations and airports to see if Steven had traveled out of the area but found nothing to indicate he had.

One of Steven's cousins created a Facebook page concerning his disappearance. People would contact her about possible sightings of Steven, and the family followed up on those that seemed the most promising. Unfortunately, none of them led to Steven.

In April 2010, the family received an anonymous tip that Steven's body was in the desert to the south of the Henderson Executive Airport. Aided by more than 70 volunteers and supervised by a Henderson Police Department detective, the family and their private investigator conducted an extensive search of the area. They found some items of clothing and a few bone fragments, but forensic tests failed to link the garments to Steven. The bones turned out to be from an animal.

Investigators combed through Steven's laptop but found nothing suspicious on it. His family was able to gain access to his email and Facebook account, but there was nothing to suggest anything was wrong. His email account was mostly filled with job application responses, and he didn't have a big social media presence. He didn't even have internet access at the home he rented; he would go to the local library to send his emails. There was nothing to suggest he had ever used the internet to meet people.

Detectives examined journal entries written shortly before Steven went missing and found no red flags. He seemed to have a positive attitude and was in no way suicidal. He was concerned about finding a job, but this was a temporary situation. The bishop at his church had indicated he would have a job opening in January and pretty much guaranteed the position to Steven.

A thorough inspection of Steven's phone records showed that he hadn't made any unusual phone calls before he went missing and there was no indication he had been talking to anyone new. There had been only one phone call made to a number no one recognized, but when police called the number they found it wasn't related to the disappearance. While Steven was distributing flyers in St. George on December 12th, he had come across two girls who were locked out of their house and had allowed them to use his phone to call their mother. With no new leads, the investigation stalled.

A year after Steven went missing, his family was no closer to finding him. They had followed up on every tip they received, but all were dead ends. The case gradually faded from the headlines, though investigators stated it was still active. The family continued to hold sporadic searches and traveled frequently to the Henderson area; they also offered a $10,000 reward for information leading to Steven.

In February 2011, the family suffered another loss. Rolf, who had searched so tirelessly for his son, was diagnosed with pneumonia on February 9th. He died in the hospital the next day, his immune system unable to fight off the bacteria. The family took time to grieve but never stopped the search for Steven.

Years went by without any movement on the case. In May 2015, Red Rock Search and Rescue became involved in the case. They organized a search of the hill areas outside Henderson, covering a 25-square-mile area. Members of the non-profit organization believed that Steven had traveled to the Henderson area to commit suicide and that he would have gone to higher ground to do so. While the family didn't necessarily endorse the suicide idea, they were happy that the group was going to conduct another search. Unfortunately, nothing connected to Steven was found.

There have been many theories put forth as possible explanations for Steven's disappearance. Some are more easily dismissed than others: Josh Powell's family tried to convince police that Susan Cox Powell was missing because she ran off with Steven. There is absolutely nothing to suggest Steven and Susan ever met, and though they disappeared within a week of each other their last known locations were 400 miles apart. Josh Powell would later kill both his children and commit suicide; he is believed to have murdered Susan as well.

Many people have suggested that Steven committed suicide due to his financial situation. He was under a lot of financial stress but according to his family, he was staying positive and showed no signs of being depressed. When he is seen walking past the surveillance camera in Henderson, he seems to be walking with a purpose. It looks like he's on his way to a job interview or another planned meeting. He doesn't look like someone about to kill himself, and he parked right in the middle of a residential area. He would have had to walk miles to find anywhere remote enough for him to commit suicide undetected.

Steven is definitely carrying something in his hand as he walks down the street. His father believed it could be a resume or job application. Steven waited in his car until exactly 12:00 pm, suggesting he may have had a noon appointment with someone. Yet there is nothing in his email or phone records to indicate he made plans to meet anyone, though it could have been arranged through a friend.

If Steven did have a job interview or other type of appointment, what happened to him? He never made it back to his car, and police found nothing to indicate Steven was the kind of person who would voluntarily leave. He was extremely close with his family, was excited about the upcoming holiday, and had already started doing some of his Christmas shopping.

Some people have suggested that Steven, desperate for money, got caught up in drug dealing as a way to make some quick cash. He did a lot of driving in the days leading up to his disappearance; his actions made some think he was working as a drug courier. His father considered this possibility and had two different narcotics dogs go over Steven's car. They showed no reaction at all, leading their handler to conclude that the car had never been used to transport drugs.

Foul play seems highly likely. In December 2020, police released close to 200 pages of documents pertaining to the case, providing a small glimpse of what went on behind the scenes in the earliest days of the investigation. Although the surveillance footage doesn't show which house Steven actually entered, police seemed to focus on one house in particular and made numerous attempts to speak with the people who lived there. At least one neighbor noted suspicious activity at this particular house on the day Steven went missing, and the occupants moved away shortly afterward. It's possible they had a hand in Steven's disappearance, though police have never named any suspects.

Although Steven's family continues to cling to the hope that he's still alive, they know there is little chance this story will have a happy ending. They continue searching, however, and are hopeful they will one day know what happened to Steven.

Steven Koecher was 30 years old when he went missing in 2009. He has blond hair and blue eyes, and at the time of his disappearance, he was 5 feet 10 inches tall and weighed 180 pounds. He has a birthmark on his abdomen and a surgical scar behind each ear. When last seen, he was wearing a white button-down shirt, jeans or Dockers, white sneakers, and a hooded sweatshirt. If you have any information about Steven, please call the St. George Police Department at 435-627-4300

Bianca Lebron

Bianca Lebron was a happy and outgoing 10-year-old girl when she went missing on November 7, 2001. It started out like a normal Wednesday at her home in Bridgeport, Connecticut. Bianca, a fifth-grade student at Elias Howe School, was in an excited mood when she arrived at school. As she stood outside the school with her teacher and classmates, she announced that her uncle was going to take her to the mall to go shopping that day.

The class was in line waiting to go inside the building at 8:30 am when they saw a brown van pull over next to the school. When the driver got out, Bianca clearly recognized him. Hopping up and down, Bianca excitedly told the group that the man driving the van was her uncle. She urged a couple of her friends to come along on the shopping trip, but they refused. Everyone watched as Bianca left the schoolyard and ran over to the van, then jumped inside. Bianca gave her classmates a final wave as the van pulled away. It was the last time the little girl would ever be seen.

Although Bianca's teacher had seen her when she arrived that morning, he didn't say anything when Bianca said she was leaving. Instead, he simply marked her down as being absent. The school did not call Bianca's home, so her mother and stepfather weren't aware of the fact that Bianca was not in class. Her mother, Carmelita Torres, was only slightly concerned when Bianca didn't return home by 4:30 pm; she was a personable girl and had a tendency to lose track of time while chatting with her friends. She knew she was supposed to call home if she stopped by a friend's house but would sometimes forget to do so.

By 8:30 pm, her family was starting to panic. They began calling her friends to see if any of them had been with Bianca after school. When they were told that Bianca hadn't attended class that day, they were stunned. They called the Bridgeport Police Department and reported her missing.

After learning from students that Bianca had been seen getting into a van with a man she referred to as her uncle, detectives initially assumed the entire thing was just a big misunderstanding. Carmelita informed the detectives that Bianca had no uncles, and no one in the family was aware of anyone who had a brown van. Bianca may have known the person who picked her up, but he certainly wasn't part of their family.

According to witnesses, a Hispanic man in his twenties was driving the van. He had a black afro and long sideburns, a prominent nose, and scratches on both of his cheeks. He was wearing a blue pullover, jeans, and scuffed brown Timberland boots. No one in Bianca's family matched that description, and they struggled to understand how Bianca's teacher could have allowed her to leave with the man.

Bianca was one of four children and was known for being friendly to everyone she met. She was confident and outspoken, and was an excellent student who enjoyed school. According to Carmelita, the 10-year-old was just starting to show an interest in boys but was too young to have had any serious relationships. Some of Bianca's friends, however, told detectives that Bianca had a "secret relationship" with an older male. They had seen Bianca with the man numerous times, and one friend claimed she saw them holding hands and kissing. They believed this was the same man who had picked her up from school. None of Bianca's friends were able to name the man.

After speaking with numerous witnesses and family members, detectives were convinced Bianca had indeed been abducted, but they had few leads to follow. They released a composite sketch of the suspect and described his van as brown and beige with several areas where the paint had been sanded off, chrome trim on the side, and tinted windows. Despite Bianca's young age, the abduction received very little media coverage; she went missing on Wednesday and the story didn't make the news until Saturday. Bianca's family did what they could to raise awareness about the case; her stepfather spent hours traveling around Bridgeport to hang up missing posters. Bianca's biological father also joined in the search, appearing at several press conferences with Carmelita to plead for the return of their daughter.

In December, police got a tip that a child matching Bianca's description had been seen in Pittsburgh. Carmelita's hopes soared, but officials in Pennsylvania looked into the sighting and were unable to confirm it was Bianca. Although tips would continue to trickle in, the case slowly went cold.

Two years after Bianca went missing, police got a tip that led to them questioning 20-year-old Jason Lara. Jason had lived in Bridgeport until a month after Bianca disappeared, when he suddenly moved to Fort Myers, Florida. Bianca had known Jason because his mother was dating Bianca's great-uncle, and Jason matched the description of the man who had taken Bianca. He also had access to a brown van during the time he lived in Bridgeport. He vehemently denied any involvement in the case, but some of Bianca's friends were adamant that Jason was the man who Bianca had been seen kissing. His girlfriend, who had been dating him for three years, said that the rumors of Jason being in any kind of relationship with Bianca were ludicrous.

Jason, who had been using the name Jason Gonzalez when he lived in Bridgeport, was wanted on a forgery charge, so he was arrested and brought back to Connecticut. While he was in custody, he was interviewed extensively by detectives about Bianca's disappearance. He continued to deny any involvement with her, and detectives were unable to find any hard evidence connecting him to the case.

In 2009, police received a tip from a confidential informant that Bianca had been killed and buried in Seaside Park in Bridgeport. Investigators dug up a 1,000-square-foot section of the park looking for any evidence to back up this claim but found nothing related to the case.

The school district in Bridgeport was highly criticized for allowing Bianca to leave school property. In the immediate aftermath of the disappearance, Bianca's teacher was suspended for not confirming that she had permission to leave school that morning. The school also made several changes to improve security, including having a police officer monitor the outside of the school during arrival and dismissal times. None of these would help ease Carmelita's rage towards the school, however, and she had Bianca declared dead seven years after she went missing. She then filed a lawsuit against the city, alleging that it was their negligence that led to Bianca's death. The case never went to trial. Instead, a settlement was reached requiring the city to pay $750,000 to the family.

According to investigators, Bianca's case remains active, but they have not had any new leads in several years. While they admit that finding her alive seems like a long shot, they don't have any solid evidence to prove she is dead and continue to hope that someone will call with the information they need to solve the case.

Bianca Lebron was just 10 years old when she went missing from Bridgeport, Connecticut in November 2001. She has brown hair, hazel eyes, and a birthmark on her forehead. At the time of her disappearance, she was 4 feet 11 inches tall and weighed 115 pounds. She was last seen wearing beige pants, a camouflage shirt, a blue denim jacket, and black boots. If you have any information on Bianca, please call the Bridgeport Police at 203-576-7671.

Melissa McGuinn

Melissa McGuinn was the first child of Robert and Becky McGuinn, born on August 3, 1987. The couple had been living in Louisiana when Becky learned she was pregnant, but moved to Trenton, New Jersey shortly before Melissa was born. They shared a rental house on Lamberton Street with another couple, Rob Ashley and his common-law wife, Wanda Reed. Robert and Rob were co-workers and had worked together in Louisiana before relocating to New Jersey.

By March 1988, the two couples had settled into a comfortable routine. Wanda had given birth to a son in January, and she and Becky assisted each other with raising their children. Although Wanda was a 30-year-old mother, she had a developmental disorder and functioned at the level of a 5-year-old. It's doubtful she had the legal capacity to consent to marriage or sex, but this apparently didn't bother Rob Ashley.

On the evening of March 5, 1988, the two couples and their infants attended a party being held by a neighbor. There were several other children at the party, and they took a liking to Melissa. At 7 months old, she didn't know how to walk or talk yet, but the kids enjoyed getting her to smile and laugh at them. They paid little attention to Wanda's son, who slept through most of the party. Wanda seemed to take offense to this, and mumbled angrily while gesturing first at her son and then at the other children. It was clear she didn't like Melissa getting all the attention while her son was ignored, and she eventually picked up her son and went home.

Everything seemed perfectly normal the next morning. The men had already left for work when Wanda knocked on Becky's bedroom door around 8:30 am. As part of their daily routine, Wanda would take Melissa downstairs and watch her while Becky got dressed. It appeared Wanda had gotten over her anger from the night before, so Becky had no qualms about handing over Melissa. She then shut her bedroom door and lit a cigarette as she tried to decide what she wanted to wear that day. She was only halfway through her cigarette when she suddenly heard a loud commotion coming from the first floor.

Becky opened her bedroom door and was surprised to see one of her neighbors bounding up the staircase. The woman seemed frantic and asked Becky where Melissa was. Becky, confused, told her neighbor that Wanda had her. Then she realized that Wanda was trailing behind the neighbor, and Melissa was nowhere in sight. Wanda mumbled something about losing the baby, and Becky felt like her heart had been ripped out of her chest.

According to the neighbor, Wanda had approached her outside and told her that Melissa had been kidnapped. Becky ran downstairs in a panic and frantically searched for her daughter. She quickly realized that Melissa was not in the house. Wanda knew she wasn't allowed to take Melissa outside unless she asked Becky for permission first; until that morning, it was a rule she had always obeyed.

Becky called the police while the neighbor searched outside for any sign of Melissa. By the time the first Trenton police officer arrived at the scene, Becky was hysterical. The officer soon realized that attempting to question Wanda was useless; her story kept changing and it was clear she didn't have the mental capacity to understand the gravity of the situation. She simply wasn't sure what she had done with the baby and gave a different answer each time the officer asked her about it. Whatever had happened, the officer knew he needed backup. He called for more units on the scene to initiate a search for the missing child, and he told Becky and Wanda they needed to go to the police station to give formal statements.

Becky placed a frantic call to her husband and told him to meet her at the police station. While she was waiting to give her statement, she suddenly felt overwhelmed with anger about the situation. Rage flooded out any semblance of common sense and she grabbed a stapler and launched herself at Wanda, perhaps thinking she could beat the truth out of her. It took several police officers to pull her away from Wanda.

While detectives were busy trying to piece together what had occurred that morning, patrol officers were conducting a large-scale search for Melissa. Wanda initially claimed that a black man had jumped out of a red car, knocked her down, and taken Melissa. It wasn't much to go on, and police soon realized just how many black men drove red cars in the city of Trenton. For the next few hours, they stopped each one they encountered. Around noon, officers were notified that Wanda had changed her story and now claimed that Melissa had been thrown into the Delaware River.

Police immediately switched their focus to the river. Unfortunately, at this point, Melissa had been missing for three hours. If Wanda had thrown her into the river, her chances of still being alive were essentially nonexistent. Although it was a calm day and the river's current was slow, the water temperature was just 38 degrees. Hypothermia was a real concern.

The Delaware River was up to 25 feet deep in parts, though many areas were much shallower. Divers were sent to search the deepest areas, while firefighters dragged nets along the shallow areas. They spent more than 7 hours combing through the river and its banks, reluctantly stopping when it got too dark to see. They found nothing to indicate Melissa was in the river.

At daybreak, the search continued. They expanded the search area, both in the water and on land. Police went door-to-door interviewing residents and handing out flyers. They combed through each abandoned building in the area. Tracking dogs were brought in, and helicopter crews flew over the Delaware River, trying in vain to find something that would point them to Melissa.

At a press conference, Robert and Becky pleaded with the public to keep an eye out for Melissa. They were convinced their daughter had been kidnapped. Police weren't so sure. Although they no longer believed Wanda's initial story about the black man in a red car, they admitted they had no idea what had happened to the baby. It was beginning to look like she wasn't going to be found in the river, though. Considering the short amount of time between when Wanda left the house with Melissa and when the neighbor came in looking for her, it didn't seem possible that Wanda could have made it to the river and back. It normally took her about 10 minutes to walk there and another 10 minutes to walk back. Wanda returned before Becky had been able to smoke an entire cigarette. There simply hadn't been enough time.

When questioned again, Wanda told detectives that she had sold Melissa to a neighbor for either $200 or an equivalent amount of drugs. This was the same neighbor who helped Becky look for Melissa the morning she went missing. Police followed up with her and were confident that she had nothing to do with Melissa's disappearance.

Investigators weren't sure if Melissa had been the victim of foul play or not. Although they had enough evidence to charge Wanda with kidnapping, it wasn't clear that she had the mental capacity to be held criminally responsible. They took her into custody but turned her over to a mental health agency in Ewing, New Jersey for a psychiatric evaluation. With Rob Ashley's consent, the State Division of Youth and Family Services took custody of their infant son.

The search for Melissa continued over the next few days, eventually covering a distance of 15 blocks in each direction. Every resident in that area had been interviewed and all empty buildings had been searched, but investigators were no closer to finding Melissa.

After she went through a 30-day evaluation at a mental health facility, Wanda was deemed mentally incompetent and unfit to stand trial. All the charges against her were dropped and the case was dismissed.

Robert and Becky McGuinn eventually moved to Arkansas and had three more children, all boys. They continued to believe that Melissa had been abducted and was still alive, likely unaware of the fact that she had been kidnapped as a baby. Unfortunately, Robert died in 2008 without ever knowing what happened to his daughter. Becky has continued to search for her and is hopeful that they will be reunited one day.

Over the years, investigators have done DNA tests on at least four women they believed could be Melissa but all the tests came back negative. Detectives believe there is a good chance Melissa is still alive but has no idea about her past. They continue to follow up on all leads they receive and are hopeful that the case will one day be solved.

Melissa McGuinn was just 7 months old when she went missing from Trenton, New Jersey in March 1988. She has reddish blonde hair and blue eyes, and at the time of her disappearance, she was just 28 inches tall and weighed 16 pounds. She was last seen wearing white quilted overalls with a flower pattern, a dark pink hooded sweater, and pink socks. If you have any information about Melissa, please contact the Trenton Police Department at 609-989-4144.

Kristen Modafferi

Kristen Modafferi was planning to have the best summer of her life. She had just finished her freshman year at North Carolina State University and was enrolled in a summer photography class at the University of California at Berkeley. Her parents hadn't been thrilled at the thought of their daughter spending a summer so far away from home, but Kristen wanted to prove she could support herself without their help. She searched the internet and found a room to rent in an old Victorian home in Oakland, and arrived in California on June 1, 1997.

Within a few days of her arrival, Kristen managed to secure two part-time jobs; the combined income would allow her to easily pay all her bills. She started working right away and spent her afternoons exploring the city. She worked her normal shift at Spinelli's coffee shop in the Crocker Galleria on June 23rd, and when her shift was over she asked her coworkers for directions to Baker Beach, which was located near Land's End Beach and was a popular spot for tourists. Her photography class was starting the next day, and she wanted to take some pictures there ahead of time. Her coworkers explained how to get there on public transportation, and Kristen was confident she could find her way. She left the coffee shop at 3:00 pm, but she didn't immediately leave the Galleria. Some of her coworkers saw her on the second floor of the building around 3:45 pm. She was talking with a blonde woman at the time; no one recognized the woman and they weren't sure if Kristen left the Galleria with her or not.

Kristen loved to travel and explore new places, and she was always taking short day trips around San Francisco. None of her housemates were too concerned when she didn't return home that night, as she had been gone overnight at least once before. They were unaware that Kristen hadn't attended the first day of her photography class; it wasn't until she missed her next scheduled shift at Spinelli's that they realized something was wrong.

Kristen was known as a brilliant student and a dependable worker. She had skipped a grade in elementary school, but the fact that she was a year younger than her classmates never affected her. She got straight As all through school and a nearly perfect score on her SATs. When she graduated from Providence High School in 1996, she was awarded a Park Scholarship, which covered her tuition for four years. Only the brightest and best students were selected to be Park Scholars, and Kristen thrived in the program. She was an industrial design major and achieved straight As during her first two semesters at the University.

Although Kristen had traveled a lot with her family and had gone to Russia on a school trip, this summer marked her first extended trip away from her parents. She had been able to visit them often when she was at North Carolina State, and it had taken a lot of persuasion before they agreed to let her go to California for the entire summer. During her first three weeks there, she called home on a regular basis and told them she was having a great time. She had made some new friends and was doing a lot of sightseeing.

Bob and Debbie Modafferi were pleased that Kristen seemed to be doing so well in San Francisco, and they were just starting to grow comfortable with the idea of her being so far away when she suddenly stopped calling home. They tried to shrug it off the first time they were unable to reach her, reminding themselves that her class was starting on June 24th and she was likely busy. Bob called the house on June 25th and left a message with one of her housemates, who promised to have Kristen call her parents when she got home. By the next morning, there was still no sign of Kristen, and her housemates were starting to worry. After speaking with some of her coworkers and learning that no one had heard from Kristen in more than 48 hours, they knew they had a problem. One of them called Kristen's parents and explained that no one had seen Kristen for a couple of days and that they were calling the police to report her missing.

Oakland Police interviewed Kristen's coworkers at Spinelli's and learned that she had planned to go to the beach on the day she was last seen. They weren't sure of her exact destination but mentioned that they thought she was going to take pictures around Land's End Beach. Kristen had not told them if she planned to go alone or not; although a couple of people saw her talking to a woman before she left the mall, her manager was fairly certain he saw Kristen leave the mall by herself.

While the Oakland Police continued interviewing people who had known Kristen, dozens of San Francisco police officers and National Park Service rangers began searching the beach areas where Kristen might have gone. Using bloodhounds, they were able to determine that Kristen had left the Galleria and walked to a nearby bus stop where she would have been able to get a bus to the beach areas. Bloodhounds were able to pick up her scent at Ocean Beach, a popular tourist area located on the west side of San Francisco. The water there was extremely rough and cold, so it wasn't a beach where people went to swim but many people stopped by because of its panoramic views of the coastline.

From Ocean Beach, the bloodhounds followed Kristen's scent to the Cliff House, a restaurant and pub that also had a gift shop that many tourists visited. There was a viewing area where people could gather to watch sea lions swim and sun themselves on some nearby rocks; it's likely that Kristen stopped there to take a few pictures. From there, bloodhounds traced her path through the Sutro Baths and then finally to a steep cliff overlooking the ocean. It was a very scenic area and looked like a perfect place to take pictures, but they couldn't find anyone who remembered seeing the missing girl there.

Searchers were unable to find any sign of Kristen, and there were fears that she might have fallen off the cliffside and drowned. Rogue waves had been known to knock unsuspecting people off of rocks in the area, and being swept out to sea was a real danger. Yet the area was normally crowded with people, and police believed that someone would have seen Kristen if she had fallen into the water in this area.

They considered the possibility that she had been abducted, but the fact that there were so many people in the area made them believe it would have been difficult for someone to take her by force without being noticed. They tried to learn the identity of the blonde woman seen with Kristen in the Galleria on the day she disappeared, but they had no real description of her; witnesses recalled only that she had been blonde and carrying a green backpack.

Bob and Debbie arrived in San Francisco the following day to assist in the search for their daughter.

Police told them that they had no signs of foul play and were considering the possibility that Kristen had disappeared voluntarily, but her parents were adamant that Kristen was not the kind of person who would ever run away. She was already spending a summer away from home, there was no need for her to run anywhere. She was excited about her photography class and already looking forward to her sophomore year at North Carolina State University. There was no way she would have walked away from everything in her life.

Although Kristen was a brilliant young woman, she had a trusting nature and was not at all street-smart. Coworkers told police about an incident earlier that summer that concerned them. Kristen had attended a concert at the Shoreline Amphitheater in Mountainview one evening, and when the concert was over she missed the last train back to Oakland. She decided that she was going to spend the night on a bench in the train station, but a young man she met at the concert told her that wasn't a safe idea. Kristen agreed to go with him to his brother's house, where she spent the night on a couch. The young man then drove her to work the following morning and had visited her at work a few times since then. Police were able to locate the man and determine that he had nothing to do with Kristen's disappearance, but the incident troubled police. Kristen had been lucky the night of the concert; she ran into a genuine good Samaritan who made sure she got home safely. If she had done something like that again, she might have trusted the wrong person.

Kristen's family offered a $10,000 reward for information about her whereabouts, and tips continued to be called in, but detectives were unable to develop any solid leads. Family and friends printed missing posters and distributed them all over the Bay area, and even considered using psychics to help find her. As the weeks went by, tips started to dwindle and Bob and Debbie feared that the public was losing interest in the case. They decided that they needed to gain national attention so they could expand the search.

Kristen's fellow Park Scholars at North Carolina State University were devastated by her disappearance. They were a tight-knit group and missed her presence when classes started in the fall. They were determined to make sure that she wasn't forgotten, and soon the entire campus was covered with flyers about their missing friend. They hung up yellow ribbons and missing posters throughout the entire city of Charlotte.

In January 1998, the Park Scholars came up with an inventive way to get Kristen's case on national television. ESPN televised the university's basketball games, so they decided to launch a massive yellow ribbon campaign and hand out ribbons at one of the basketball games. Every spectator was given a ribbon to wear; although NCAA rules prevented the players themselves from wearing the ribbons during the game, their coach made sure to wear one, and before the game was over the coach of the opposing team made sure he got one as well. Their ploy worked; the sea of yellow ribbons had fans watching the game from their homes calling ESPN to see what they were about, and the sportscasters spent a few minutes talking about Kristen's disappearance.

By May 1998, police admitted that they were certain that Kristen had been the victim of foul play, but they were at a standstill when it came to determining exactly what happened. As they went back through all the evidence that was collected during the investigation, they noticed something taken from Kristen's room that they hadn't seen before in a newspaper found in Kristen's trash can. They discovered that she had circled a personal ad in one of the local papers; upon reading the ad, they believed that Kristen may have been the author.

The Bay Guardian had done a special promotion where ads could be taken out for free the week of June 11th, and it appeared Kristen may have taken advantage of this. The ad read "Female seeking friend(s) to share activities, who enjoy music, photography, working out, walks, coffee, or simply exploring the Bay Area. Interested, call me!"

Unfortunately, by the time police picked up on the potential significance of the ad, the paper had gotten a new computer system and had purged all its old files. There was no way to confirm if Kristen had taken out the ad or perhaps responded to it, but detectives wondered if the blonde woman seen with Kristen on the day she went missing may have been someone she met through the ad. They renewed their plea for information about the woman, but she was never identified.

Kristen's parents returned to San Francisco numerous times over the next year, each time distributing new flyers about the case and making sure people knew about the reward. In July 1998 they increased the reward to $25,000, hoping the larger amount would bring in more potential tips. Police stated that they believed more than one person knew what happened to Kristen, and they urged anyone who knew anything to come forward, even if they chose to do so anonymously.

That fall, Bob and Debbie appeared on the Maury Povich show, desperate to make sure that their daughter's case remained in the public eye. They once again doubled the reward, offering $50,000 for any information leading to Kristen or the people responsible for her disappearance.

Although they were still hoping that she was alive, they knew that she had most likely run into foul play and they wanted the people who took her from them to be held responsible. An anonymous donor donated 20 billboards around the San Francisco area to the family, and they used them to publicize the new reward.

Detectives continued to follow up on all the leads that were called in, but they felt like they were going in circles. Although they were convinced that Kristen had not made it back from the beach that day, they had no evidence pointing to any possible suspects. This changed in May 1999, when police announced that they were looking for a 37-year-old man named Jon Onuma for questioning in Kristen's disappearance. He had been in the San Francisco area at the time she went missing, but had recently left the area and they were trying to locate him.

Jon Onuma had been on police radar since the early days of the investigation, when he called in a tip claiming that he knew who killed Kristen and where they had dumped her body. Although he had refused to give his name, police were able to trace the tip back to him, and he finally admitted that he was the person who called. He claimed two women that he knew were responsible for killing Kristen; police interviewed both women and determined that they were not involved in Kristen's case. They had worked at a local YMCA with Jon's wife and had been responsible for getting her fired. Jon had called and said they were the killers as a way of getting revenge on them. With nothing connecting Jon to the disappearance, police initially chalked the incident up to a failed revenge attempt and nothing more.

In the spring of 1998, three separate women came forward to police, accusing Jon Onuma of various crimes against them, ranging from sexual assault to kidnapping.

One of the women claimed that Jon had told her that he was going to kill her, and then she would know what happened to Kristen Modafferi. She fled, but told police that she believed Jon had been serious and that he was responsible for Kristen's disappearance. Detectives were anxious to take another look at Onuma, but he had left California and no one knew where he was living.

The television show "America's Most Wanted" aired a segment about the case, and asked for viewers to call in if they had any knowledge of the case or where Jon Onuma could be found. More than 70 people called in after seeing the show, and one of them was able to lead detectives to Onuma. He was living with his girlfriend in Hawaii, though police were certain that he had returned to the Bay area at least once since in recent days.

Onuma called detectives and spoke to them on the phone for about an hour, steadfastly denying any involvement in the case. He agreed to fly to California and take a lie detector test as well. Whatever information they learned from him, it didn't lead to any criminal charges against him in connection with Kristen's case. Detectives have never officially cleared him as a suspect but said only that they had no evidence linking him to Kristen.

The FBI opened a criminal kidnapping investigation into Kristen's disappearance in 2006 and noted that they have had some persons of interest over the years, but there has never been any evidence that would lead to criminal charges. Detectives continue to look into any tips that are called in, but the case has not seen much progress in the last few years.

Kristen's parents remain dedicated to finding their daughter and have hired a private investigator to help them in their search. In 2015, a cadaver dog was taken to the home where Kristen lived in Oakland, and the private detective said that the dog seemed to pick up the scent of human remains in the basement of the home. At the time Kristen lived there, the house next to hers was being used as a halfway house for parole violators, and the private detective believes that this lead should have been looked at more closely in the days immediately following the investigation. To date, nothing has been found in the home that directly connects to Kristen.

Kristen Deborah Modafferi was 18 years old when she went missing from San Francisco, California in June 1997. She has brown eyes and dark brown hair, and has deep dimples in both cheeks when she smiles. At the time of her disappearance, she was 5 feet 8 inches tall and weighed 140 pounds. She was last seen wearing tan pants, a black Spinelli's t-shirt, a blue plaid flannel shirt, and Fly London sneakers. She was carrying a green Jansport backpack with two library books inside as well as her camera. If you have any information on Kristen, please contact the Oakland Police Department at 510-238-3641.

Morgan Nick

Morgan Nick was starting to get restless. For the past hour and a half, the 6-year-old had been sitting with her mother at a Little League game in Alma, Arkansas. For a while, she amused herself by repeatedly untying her mother's shoelaces when she wasn't looking, but her giggling kept giving her away. When two of her friends stopped and asked if she wanted to play with them, she was happy for the distraction. It took a bit of pleading before her mother agreed to let her, but once she had permission she happily bounded down the bleachers and followed her friends to a sandy area near the parking lot. One minute, she was less than 150 feet away from her mother and the rest of the 300 people attending the Little League game. The next minute, she was gone. It was June 9, 1995, and the tiny town of Alma would never be the same.

Morgan lived in Ozark, Arkansas with her mom, Colleen Nick, and two younger siblings. She tended to be shy around people she didn't know, but she enjoyed making people laugh and had an infectious smile. She took her role as big sister seriously; she was just learning to read and would try to read bedtime stories to her younger brother each night. In many ways, she was a typical little girl who loved cats, bubblegum, and the color pink. Although her friends had tried to get her to join them in track and field when she was in first grade, she quit after one practice. She hadn't realized how sweaty running would make her, and she hated to sweat. She had her mom sign her up for Girl Scouts instead, preferring to sit inside and do arts and crafts. She loved being a Girl Scout and even wore her bright green Girl Scout shirt to the Little League game.

Colleen had been invited to attend the game by friends who had a child on the team. Although Alma was 30 miles from Ozark, Colleen decided to make the trip. Morgan's siblings, 3-year-old Logan and 1-year-old Taryn, were too young to enjoy the game, so Colleen left them at home with her mother. She had never been to the Alma Little League field before, but it was located near I-40 and easy to find. After parking in the lot adjoining the field, she and Morgan joined her friends on the bleachers and settled in to watch the game.

Not long after they arrived, Morgan saw two children that she knew, 8-year-old Jessica and 10-year-old Tye. They asked Morgan if she wanted to play with them, but she told them she wanted to stay in the bleachers with her mother. For the next hour, she sat and watched the game while Colleen chatted with her friends. When she got bored of baseball and adult conversation, she started untying her mother's sneakers. As soon as Colleen retied them, Morgan would untie them again. Eventually, even this game lost its appeal.

After the sun set, Jessica and Tye returned to the bleachers and asked Morgan if she wanted to catch fireflies with them. Morgan asked her mother if she could, but Colleen told her she didn't think it was a good idea. It was dark, the game was almost over, and she was unfamiliar with the park. As Morgan began to plead with her mother, Colleen's friends jumped in and assured Colleen it was perfectly safe. Children would always roam around freely at the park and nothing had ever happened to any of them. Reluctantly, Colleen gave Morgan permission. After giving her mom a quick hug and kiss, the little girl left with her friends.

Colleen relaxed a little when she realized she could see Morgan from where she was sitting. The three children had climbed a small sandy hill overlooking the parking lot and were chasing after fireflies. Colleen glanced over three or four times in the next 10 minutes; the children were in the same place each time. As the baseball game finished up, the three children abandoned their hunt for fireflies. They trudged back to the parking lot, stopping briefly to empty sand out of their shoes. As Colleen made her way to the parking lot, she saw Jessica and Tye heading back toward the field. They told her when they left Morgan, she had been leaning on Colleen's car trying to get all the sand out of her sneakers. They assumed she was going to wait there for her mother. Colleen approached her car but saw no sign of Morgan. She circled the car, willing herself not to panic. She frantically scanned the thinning crowd for her daughter, but it only took seconds for her to realize that Morgan was gone. It was a small ball field, and there was nowhere for a child to hide. Morgan was timid in new situations, and Colleen knew she wouldn't have wandered off on her own. If she was missing, someone must have taken her.

The police were called, and an officer from the Alma Police Department was on the scene in minutes. Tye and Jessica were the last people to see Morgan, and when the officer spoke with them, he immediately realized the situation was serious. They told the officer a man in the parking lot had been talking to them earlier, and he had been watching them while they were chasing fireflies. When they were dumping the sand out of their shoes, they saw him leaning on his pickup truck, still watching them. He and his truck vanished from the parking lot at the same time Morgan went missing.

The children may not have understood the significance of seeing this man, but the officer did. Earlier in the day, a man in a red pickup truck had tried to abduct a 4-year-old girl from a laundromat in Alma. The child's mother had realized what was going on and was able to prevent him from taking her daughter, but the man was long gone by the time police were notified of the incident. It was possible this same man had taken Morgan. The responding officer immediately called for backup.

Before the weekend was over, the FBI and the Arkansas State Police joined the investigation. They launched a massive search for Morgan, with searchers on foot, horseback, and in the air scouring the area for anything related to the case. They created a composite sketch of the man Jessica and Tye had seen; by Sunday there would be a nationwide manhunt for him and his truck. The man was described as being 23 to 38 years old, around 6 feet tall and 180 pounds. He had dark or salt & pepper hair, a mustache, and a short beard. He had been wearing only a pair of cut-off jean shorts and had a hairy chest. The children thought he had a hillbilly-type accent. His truck had been an old red Ford pickup with a white camper shell. The camper had possible damage on its right rear side and was about four inches too short for the truck. The truck had a short wheelbase, dull, old-looking paint, and possibly an Arkansas license plate. No one had actually seen the man abduct Morgan, but he was the best suspect they had and they poured most of their resources into finding him.

Detectives were assigned to interview Morgan's family, friends, and the 300 people who had attended the Little League game. As in all missing children investigations, they started with the parents. Collen and

John Nick, Morgan's father, had divorced six months earlier, but they had a cordial relationship and there was no ongoing custody battle between them. Detectives were able to quickly rule them out as suspects.

The small town of Alma rallied around the Nick family and did everything possible to assist in the search. Colleen refused to go home to Ozark without her daughter, so she and her family spent the first six weeks of the search living in Alma's volunteer firehouse. Located directly across the street from the police station, the firehouse would become the unofficial base for the search. Pink ribbons went up all over town to remind people Morgan was still missing, and every single building displayed both Morgan's missing poster and the composite sketch of the suspect.

Police received dozens of potential sightings; they followed up on 247 reports of red trucks in the first week of the search. People called from all over Arkansas, as well as from Texas and Oklahoma. Police investigated every tip as it came in, convinced that they would soon find the truck – and driver – that would lead them to Morgan. Each lead, however, turned out to be a dead end.

Two weeks after Morgan went missing, police got a call from a man in Stuttgart, Arkansas who was certain he had seen both Morgan and her abductor. Albert Harvey had been working in his yard when he saw a man trying to break into his truck. Once the man realized someone was watching him, he ran off into a wooded area, dragging a small blonde girl behind him. Albert said the man looked just like the composite sketch of the suspect, and the blonde girl was definitely Morgan. Police were elated and immediately sent dozens of officers to Stuttgart, about 200 miles away from Alma. Albert was so certain about the identification that Morgan's parents were flown in by private jet so they could be on scene when their daughter was found.

Authorities blocked off a 6-square-mile area within Stuttgart and launched a massive search. National Guard helicopters were deployed, and officers combed through the dense brush using infrared light, search dogs, and mounted units. Countless volunteers from the surrounding community came out to offer their assistance. The weather was brutally hot and humid, and there were mosquitoes everywhere. Despite the grueling conditions, the searchers pushed on for more than 16 hours without finding anything.

John and Colleen grew more anxious with each passing hour, but detectives grew more suspicious. They brought Albert Harvey in for questioning. Even after failing two polygraph examinations administered by the FBI and the Arkansas State Police, Albert insisted he had seen Morgan and her abductor. It took two more hours of questioning before he broke down and admitted he had been lying. He had actually seen a man trying to break into his truck, but he had no idea if he looked like the potential abductor and there had never been a blonde girl with him.

Thousands of dollars had been wasted on the search effort in Stuttgart, but Albert didn't seem to appreciate the seriousness of what he had done. He told police he just got carried away and apologized to the searchers for having to put up with all the mosquitoes. He was then arrested and charged with filing a false police report. Devastated, the Nicks flew back to Alma without their daughter.

By August, leads in the case were dwindling. Although police vowed that they wouldn't stop working the case until they found Morgan, the trail was growing cold. Searches would continue to be held sporadically, and detectives still followed up on every tip they received, but nothing brought them any closer to finding Morgan. FBI profilers believed it was possible that the abductor was a professional kidnapper, someone who took children and then sold them on the black market.

Colleen refused to give up on the search and was confident that Morgan was out there somewhere waiting to be found. Morgan's siblings were too young to fully understand what was going on; Logan couldn't understand how his mother had managed to lose his sister and demanded she go out and find her. He was afraid that the people who had Morgan would be mean to her. He worried that they would yell at her all the time and refuse to take her out for pizza. To a 3-year-old, that was the worst fate imaginable.

Years went by, and the investigation stalled. Then, in January 2002, a new tip that came in led police to investigate a property in Logan County, Arkansas. Though they released no information about the tip itself, they said it was specific enough that they felt a search was justified. They brought search dogs to the property and then spent a day digging up different sections, but found nothing.

In November 2010, federal investigators searched a vacant house in Spiro, Oklahoma after receiving a tip from a confidential informant. Spiro was about 25 miles from Alma, and the property they searched had once belonged to a convicted child molester who was currently in jail. Although investigators had nothing linking the man to Morgan's disappearance, they searched through the home looking for possible DNA evidence that might indicate Morgan had been there. Unfortunately, they didn't uncover anything related to the case.

In December 2017, investigators returned to the same house in Spiro. This time, their search focused on a well located on the property. They dug around the property for 10 hours before concluding there was nothing to be found. This was the last major search pertaining to Morgan's disappearance. Her case remains open, and police are still hopeful that they will one day get the tip they need to finally learn what happened to Morgan.

In November 2021, the FBI announced that they had a suspect in the case, a man named Billy Jack Lincks. He had been charged with a sex crime in 1992 and was arrested again in August 1995 and convicted of sexual indecency after attempting to abduct an 11-year-old girl in Van Buren, Arkansas – just eight miles away from the baseball field where Morgan was last seen. The victim in that case told investigators that Lincks had been driving a red pickup truck at the time of the crime. Unfortunately for investigators, Billy Jack Lincks died in 2000, taking whatever he might have known about Morgan to his grave.

Morgan's family never stopped searching for her. In 1996, Colleen started the Morgan Nick Foundation. Her main focus remained finding Morgan, but she also lobbied for changes in how missing children cases were handled and worked with legislators to enact laws geared towards child safety. The foundation works to educate children about the dangers of child abduction and offers crisis management to families of missing children. For more information, visit: https://morgannickfoundation.com/

Morgan Nick was just 6 years old when she disappeared from Alma, Arkansas in June 1995. She has blonde hair and blue eyes, and at the time of her disappearance, she was 4 feet tall and weighed 55 pounds. She had five visible silver caps on her molars that were due to be removed in 2000. When last seen, she was wearing a green Girl Scout shirt, cut-off denim shorts, and white tennis shoes. If you have any information about Morgan, please call the Alma Police Department at 501-632-3333, the Arkansas State Police at 501-783-5795, or the FBI at 202-324-3000.

Leah Occhi

The remnants of Hurricane Andrew were headed for Tupelo, Mississippi on the morning of August 27, 1992. Vickie Yarborough arrived at her job that morning around 7:50 am, leaving her daughter home alone. Leigh, who had just celebrated her 13th birthday the previous week, had been awake but still in her nightgown when her mother left for work. School was going to be starting soon, and Leigh's grandmother was going to pick her up that day so she could attend an open house at Tupelo Middle School. Although Leigh was not a newcomer to the school – she would be starting eighth grade – the school had been completely renovated over the summer, and the open house was being held so students could tour the new building.

Less than an hour after she arrived at work, Vickie heard a severe thunderstorm warning for the area. Leigh was terrified of thunderstorms, so Vickie called home to warn her. Whenever Vickie would call Leigh, she would let the phone ring twice, hang up, then immediately redial. This ensured Leigh knew it was her mother calling and would answer the phone. On that morning, however, Leigh failed to pick up. After trying a few more times, Vickie grew concerned. She called her mother to see if she would make the five-minute drive to the house so she could check on Leigh.

Rather than wait for her mother to call her, Vickie decided to leave work and head home. She lived only a mile and a half from her office, so it only took her a few minutes to get home. Her blood ran cold when she pulled up in front of her house and saw that the garage door was wide open, and the light on the automatic door opener was lit. Since the light would turn off about five minutes after the door opener was used, it appeared someone had just left.

When Vickie got into the house, she was horrified by what she saw. There was blood smeared on one of the walls and trailed down the hallway. Yelling for Leigh, she quickly checked all the rooms in the house but couldn't find her daughter. She ran outside into the backyard, checked the shed, then came back inside and called 911.

Police arrived within minutes and immediately knew that they were not dealing with a runaway teenager. The two officers who had been dispatched made the wise decision to call for a detective to come to the house; Lead Detective Bart Aguirre received the call and headed straight to the residence. He took a cursory look around the home and noticed blood and hair on a door frame, a pool of blood on the carpet, and drops of blood leading down the hallway. Aguirre noted that the blood had not yet started to congeal, meaning it hadn't been there for very long.

Vickie showed him the nightgown Leigh had been wearing when she last saw her; it was stained with blood and had been thrown into a laundry basket. He noted that the blood appeared to have dripped down onto the nightgown, leading him to believe that it was most likely from a head injury. In the master bedroom's bathroom, there was evidence that someone had tried to clean up, leaving a pink sheen of blood on the counter. Nothing else in the home appeared to be disturbed, and there was no sign of forced entry.

Police and volunteers started searching the

surrounding area for Leigh, but the stormy weather made it difficult. Bloodhounds had no luck in picking up on a scent trail, and the weather was too bad for aerial searches. Detectives began interviewing everyone who knew Leigh, starting with immediate family. They were hoping to uncover clues that would lead them to Leigh.

Leigh had been born in Honolulu, Hawaii on August 21, 1979; she was the only child of Donald Occhi and Vickie Felton. Her parents were in the army and met when they were both stationed in California. They got married in 1977, but the honeymoon phase didn't last long and they got divorced in 1981. Vickie was in labor for 18 hours before Leigh finally made her entrance, and Donald fell in love with her the second he saw her. After the divorce, Donald was sent to Germany, but he stayed in close contact with Leigh. She even spent time with him while he was stationed in Germany, and he enjoyed taking her to some of the country's tourist attractions.

Donald and Vickie would both go on to get remarried. Vickie had married Barney Yarborough, but they had been separated for a month at the time of Leigh's disappearance. Donald and his second wife, Cathy, were living in Virginia and had two children together. Donald had been deployed to Iraq during Operation Desert Storm and had only been back in the country for about six months when his daughter went missing.

There hadn't appeared to be anything abnormal or unusual in Leigh's life in the days and weeks leading up to the disappearance. Her birthday had been six days earlier, and she celebrated with a party at a local arcade. One of her friends would later tell reporters that Leigh had been in a great mood at her party; if she had been dealing with anything out of the ordinary in her life, she hid it well.

When detectives spoke to some of Vickie's

neighbors, they described Leigh as being a friendly and intelligent child who was comfortable around adults. One neighbor recalled that, the night before Leigh vanished, she had knocked on his front door around 8:00 pm. She had been locked out of her house and wanted to know if she could wait at his home until her mother returned. She stayed for about 45 minutes, then went to the home of Mitzi Phillips, who lived directly across the street from Leigh. She was only there for about 15 minutes before she looked out the window and saw that her mother had returned home. Mitzi noted she had been very chatty and in a good mood, and she didn't get the sense there was anything wrong.

Detectives interviewed Vickie the same day that Leigh disappeared. Vickie said it had been a completely normal morning at home. When she woke up, Leigh had been in her bed, which was common when it was storming because she was afraid of thunder. Vickie got up at 6:45 am to start getting ready for work, and Leigh got up shortly after that. Vickie said she read the morning paper while she and Leigh had breakfast and talked about Leigh's plans for the day. She was going to stay in the house until her grandmother picked her up to take her to see the new middle school, and she was hoping to get Taco Bell for dinner that evening.

Vickie left the house around 7:45 am to go to work at Leggett and Platt, a manufacturing company just minutes away from her home. She told detectives she was pretty sure that she had shut the garage door when she left that morning since it was something she always did, but she had no specific recollection of doing so. She arrived at work around 7:50 am. While listening to the radio there, she learned there was a severe storm moving into the area. She told detectives that she immediately

116

grew scared when she was unable to get her daughter on the phone, and that was why she left work less than an hour after she got there. Although she had called her mother to check on Leigh, she arrived at the house before her and raced inside calling out for Leigh. After checking all over, she knew she had to get the police involved.

Despite the immediate response, searchers were unable to find any trace of Leigh. Bart Aguirre, the first detective on the scene, said that they covered a half-mile radius around the house in the first couple of hours of the search. In addition to police, around 100 volunteers also showed up to help. Aguirre believes that the rainy and windy weather prevented the dogs from being able to get a good scent.

As soon as the storm passed, a helicopter was dispatched to fly over the area. Detectives were hopeful that an aerial search might reveal evidence they had missed during the ground search, but the helicopters didn't have any luck either. Unable to find any evidence outside, detectives went back to the home and continued looking for clues there. They told the media that foul play appeared to be involved in Leigh's disappearance; although they had no suspects at that time, they had not ruled anyone out. Everyone was considered a person of interest until they had enough evidence to point in a specific direction.

Leigh had been missing for two days before Vickie called Donald Occhi with news of her disappearance. Since Vickie didn't appear to be at all emotional or upset, Donald initially believed that Leigh had left the house on her own and would quickly return. He even told Vickie to give it a couple days and see if she came back. It was such a small town, he was convinced she wouldn't be able to remain hidden for long. Recalling that day, he told a reporter "I had no idea there was blood and stuff like that. I figured she might have run off because I heard rumors that her mother and stepfather didn't treat her very well."

Donald was horrified when he learned about the condition of the home and the amount of blood that had been found. He and his wife, Cathy, made the trip to Tupelo from their home at a Virginia military base. Donald would remain in Tupelo for a month, long after his wife had to return to Virginia to go back to work and enroll their son in school. He was still drawing a paycheck from the army, and that coupled with the generosity of volunteers and a local hotel made it possible for him to stay for so long. He was grateful to the residents of Tupelo for all their support, noting that it made what was a terrible situation slightly more bearable.

To make sure every angle of the case was covered, the Tupelo Police Department created a task force on September 1st. They canvassed the area, looking for anyone who might have seen something unusual on the day Leigh went missing. While local residents desperately wanted to help find Leigh, no one had witnessed anything odd. No one recalled seeing any strange cars in the neighborhood, and no one heard anyone screaming or fighting. Of course, many of the locals had been preoccupied that morning. With Hurricane Andrew headed straight for them, most had been completing their pre-storm preparations.

On September 4th, a community college student in Booneville, Mississippi called police after seeing a girl who looked like Leigh. The child had been inside a truck that went through the drive-thru of a McDonald's. Investigators went to Booneville, located about 30 miles north of Tupelo; they were able to locate the child in question and determine it wasn't Leigh.

Vickie called police on September 9th to report getting a strange package in the mail. It was addressed to Barney Yarborough, and the postmark indicated it had been mailed from Booneville. Inside were Leigh's reading glasses. Although there was no ransom note included, the FBI joined the investigation at this point and sent the package to their crime lab for forensic analysis. Detectives were hopeful that the package might be the break they needed to solve the case. Unfortunately, technicians in the crime lab had been unable to find useful evidence. The stamps had been moistened with water, not saliva, and the package yielded no fibers, fingerprints, or DNA evidence. Bart Aguirre, one of the detectives working on the case, would later tell reporters that he believed the package had been nothing but a distraction tactic to keep police from looking for Leigh.

Three weeks after Leigh vanished, her home was sealed off and a well-known forensic expert from Hattiesburg, Mike West, was called in to go through the house. Police were tight-lipped about what, if anything, had led them to this point, and the complete results of the forensic analysis were not released to the public.

The blood that had been found throughout the home had been type O, and investigators assumed that it had come from Leigh but couldn't be sure. Detective Aguirre noted that Leigh had never been hospitalized and had never had any kind of bloodwork done, so there was nothing that could be compared to the blood found in the home.

Detective Aguirre was somewhat perplexed by Vickie's general demeanor, as she showed very little emotion about the situation. Still, he refrained from calling her a suspect in the case. He admitted that they had to depend on her for information about what had happened that morning since she was the only other person living in the home and had been the last person to see Leigh. At the very least, this made her a person of interest.

Early in the investigation, detectives gave polygraph examinations to Vickie, Barney, and Donald. The results were kept confidential for years, but authorities would later state that Barney and Donald had passed their tests and weren't considered suspects in Leigh's disappearance. The same could not be said for Vickie. She failed the first polygraph the local police gave her. The FBI then administered tests to Vickie on two separate occasions, and she failed both of these as well. Since polygraphs are not admissible as evidence in court, police can only use them as an investigative tool and can't arrest someone solely because they failed a polygraph. Vickie has continued to maintain her innocence in the case and says she only failed the tests because she was stressed out and anxious about the situation in general.

In the weeks and months following Leigh's disappearance, investigators had their hands full trying to follow up on all the rumors that were flying around town regarding the missing girl. Some people swore that Leigh had suffered from physical and sexual abuse at the hands of her stepfather and/or her mother, others claimed to know how Leigh was killed and where her body could be found. Police found themselves trying to hunt down the origins of these rumors and it distracted them from the actual investigation. It got so out of hand that the chief of police finally banned all police personnel from talking about the case, both in an official capacity and while off-duty. Violators would be hit with a two-week suspension.

Physical searches of the area continued, and police also went through a local landfill looking for possible evidence. They found nothing. As the fall hunting season got underway, they asked hunters to keep an eye out for anything unusual while they were trekking through remote areas of the county. They also performed another aerial search once the leaves began falling from trees, but had no more luck than they had over the summer.

As months went by, investigators grew more frustrated. They were certain that Leigh had been a victim of foul play, but they continued to come up empty in their search for physical evidence. Vickie, annoyed that police believed her daughter was dead, hired a private investigator to start looking the case over from the beginning. She also announced that she was raising the reward for information about Leigh from $2,000 to $5,000. Vickie seemed to harbor no resentment over the fact that police were treating her as a person of interest. She told reporters that she knew they were just doing their job, but she wished that they would focus on alternative theories instead of assuming that Leigh was already dead. Unless they found Leigh's body, Vickie said she would continue to believe she was alive.

In December, Leigh was pronounced the first-place winner of a National Guard poster contest she had entered shortly before she went missing. It was a bittersweet moment. Vickie, a member of the 155th Armored Brigade, was featured on the poster Leigh made, and it was placed on display in Jackson, Mississippi.

Leigh's case remained at a standstill throughout most of 1993. Then, there was a possible break. On November 2nd, a farmer harvesting soybeans was surprised to find a human skull in his field. He immediately called police, who did a cursory search of the area but didn't find any other bones. The skull was sent to the state medical examiner's office so pathologists could attempt to identify it using dental records. Just four days later, it was announced that the skull belonged to Leigh. Her family was heartbroken.

A recovery team was sent out to the area where the skull had been found, and a few hours later they announced that they had recovered the rest of the remains. Two days after that, residents of Tupelo were shocked when it was announced that the remains weren't Leigh's after all. The state medical examiner, Emily Ward, noted that most of the teeth had been missing from the skull when they initially received it, but insisted that they had not made any mistakes in the process. Instead, the pathologists had done the best they could with the limited evidence they had.

Dr. Ward's explanation didn't go over well with Leigh's family; they had been devastated by the mistaken identity. In August 1994, Dr. Ward's office examined the body of a murdered girl. She told the parents that the girl had been raped before she was killed, but a few days later came forward to say the girl hadn't actually been raped. Although Vickie had nothing to do with that case, she was incensed that the same office could mess up again and wrote a scathing letter to the editor of the Hattiesburg American. "Rumors, speculation, and fake reports about a loved one's fate cannot be forgotten once placed in your mind. Believe me." She went on to note that, if her dentist hadn't taken it upon himself to double-check with the medical examiner's office, the mistake wouldn't have been discovered at all.

Aside from the blood found inside the home and the eyeglasses received in the mail, there have been no clues found in Leigh's disappearance. The case is still considered an open and active investigation, and tips still come in occasionally. Barney Yarborough died years ago, but Donald is still alive and continues to hope that Leigh will be found one day. He firmly believes his daughter is dead, but would like to be able to give her a proper burial. Vickie left the Mississippi area; in 2017 she was living in Michigan with her parents. Although she insisted for years that she believed Leigh was still alive, she thinks she knows who is behind the disappearance and has come to realize that there is little chance Leigh is still alive.

Police have looked into Oscar "Mike" Kearns, the man that Vickie thinks took her daughter, but they have never found any evidence to conclusively tie him to the crime. He was a Sunday School and Vacation Bible School teacher at the church Leigh and Vickie attended, and he was someone Leigh knew fairly well. Leigh had a love of horses, and Kearns had invited her to go horseback riding on at least one occasion. He is someone that Leigh would have considered safe, so if he showed up at her door she would have had no qualms about letting him in.

While Kearns adopted the persona of a friendly and religious man, he was hiding a dark secret. In May 1993, less than nine months after Leigh went missing, Kearns drove to Memphis and kidnapped a ninth-grade girl he had met at a church function. He showed up at her home around 7:00 am, when the girl was the only person home. He told her that he was going to drive her to school, but instead took her to a remote area of DeSoto County and raped her. Then, rather than try to hide what he did, he drove the girl to her school and left. Thankfully, the girl was brave enough to immediately call police and report the crime. Kearns was arrested and pleaded guilty to the charges. He was sentenced to 24 years, but 16 years were suspended, meaning he only had to serve eight years for the crime. He ended up being released from prison in 1997 after serving less than half of that sentence. The following year, he kidnapped a couple and raped the female, landing him back in jail. Detectives tried to question him regarding Leigh's case, but his lawyer would not permit him to speak with them. There is absolutely no physical evidence linking him to the crime, but he is still considered to be a person of interest.

There are several different theories about what might have happened to Leigh. Detectives quickly ruled out the possibility that she ran away from home; if it was indeed her blood found inside the home, she would not have been able to get very far on her own. Likewise, suicide can be ruled out as her body was never found, and an accidental death is unlikely. Leigh was almost certainly abducted and murdered; the only question is who did it.

There were numerous rumors that spread throughout Tupelo shortly after Leigh went missing. There were several people who claimed that Leigh had been abused by her stepfather and/or her mother; some even said that she would show up at school all the time with bruises and black eyes. If this is the case, it was clearly never reported, as there are no records indicating that Leigh received medical treatment due to abuse injuries, and no evidence that police had any contact with the family prior to Leigh's disappearance. That doesn't mean the abuse didn't happen, but without evidence to back up the claim there is nothing that can be done.

Initially, local residents seemed to believe that Barney may have had something to do with the disappearance, but after he passed a polygraph and police said he had an alibi and fully cooperated with investigators, this rumor began to die down. There had been whispers from the very beginning that Vickie might be involved, and once police seemed to clear Barney the brunt of local suspicion was transferred to Vickie. Even those who didn't believe that she had actually committed the crime herself believed that she knew more than she was telling police.

During the initial search effort for Leigh, Donald was a very visible figure. He was willing to go to any length if it meant finding his daughter, and he took part in numerous searches. At one of these searches, a television reporter asked him if Vickie or anyone from her family had been out searching, too. The question elicited a wry smile from Donald, and he told the reporter that if any of them showed up to search it would be a complete surprise to him. Although he tried to hold back from saying anything negative about Vickie, he would later admit that he had doubts about her from the beginning. Almost immediately after he arrived in Tupelo to assist in the search, numerous people came up to him and suggested that he take a close look at Vickie because she had likely played a role in the disappearance. Donald tried to shake them off, but the thought remained in the back of his mind.

Police had their own doubts about Vickie, especially after she failed three polygraphs. Still, they were hesitant to call her a suspect. Detective Aguirre felt that Vickie's version of what had happened on the morning Leigh vanished was incomplete, and he had several questions that she was never able to answer. He also thought it was particularly odd that she left work to check on Leigh less than an hour after arriving. She had already called her mother to go to the house and check things out, and he thought it was odd that she would then race home, beating even her mother who lived only five minutes away. He noted that they had searched Vickie's car, even sending the liner from the trunk out for forensic testing, but they never found anything to indicate Vickie had used the car to transport Leigh's body.

During her initial interview with detectives on the

day of the disappearance, Vickie noted that it had been the very first day she had left Leigh alone in the house. In the same interview, she stated that, when calling Leigh, she would let the phone ring twice before hanging up and redialing. This was so Leigh would know it was her mother calling and it was safe to answer the phone. If Leigh had never been left home alone before, there would have been no need for Vickie to use this little code. The fact that Vickie would lie over something like this made police slightly suspicious of her from the start. They also questioned her timeline for the day. By her account, Leigh had only been home alone for around an hour before Vickie returned. This was a very tight timeline for someone to convince Leigh to let them into the house, attack and possibly murder her, take off her bloodstained nightgown, put her into new clothes and shoes, attempt to clean up the crime scene, and then take Leigh and flee.

Vickie's aloof demeanor during interviews made some people view her with suspicion. Some found her to be cold and uncaring, not at all how they believed that a person with a missing child should appear. While Vickie was very composed in front of news cameras, she had also been in the army where she had been trained to deal with stressful situations. As a female soldier at a time when most were male, she likely had to learn early on how to hide any emotions that could be seen as a sign of weakness. She may have simply been putting on a brave front. When Leigh's 12-year-old boyfriend called the house to speak with Leigh the day she disappeared, he recalled that Vickie had started to cry when she had to explain to the child what she meant when she told him Leigh was missing. Perhaps, since he was a child, Vickie was more comfortable letting her guard down with him.

Some people have speculated that Leigh's death

was accidental. While there is no evidence that Vickie was ever abusive to her daughter, Leigh had just turned 13. It's an age where many children start testing the limits of their parents' patience. Vickie had just separated from her husband, so it's fair to say that she may have been dealing with some emotional stress at the time. Perhaps she and Leigh got into an argument that started out as a shouting match but then escalated. The blood and hair detectives found on a doorframe were at the exact height it would have been at if Leigh's head had slammed into it. Detective Aguirre noted that there was a fist-sized pool of blood on the carpet near the door frame; he believed Leigh may have fallen down and laid there for a few minutes while bleeding heavily from a head wound. It's possible that Vickie may have shoved Leigh into the door frame during a physical altercation, not realizing the amount of damage it would actually do.

The blood pooled on the floor was fresh; Detective Aguirre noticed that it hadn't even had time to begin congealing. If the timeline provided by Vickie is correct, it's doubtful that she could have been the person responsible for Leigh's injuries. She was gone for over an hour, and blood will normally start to clot within 15 minutes. There are many variables that can change how quickly blood starts to congeal, though, so this doesn't completely rule Vickie out.

If Vickie was the person who harmed Leigh, it's unclear when she would have had time to get rid of her body. In order for the body to be hidden somewhere virtually undetectable to searchers, Vickie would have likely needed another person to help. Barney seems like a likely choice, but he had an alibi for that morning and passed a polygraph. She could have enlisted the help of her mother, but there has never been any evidence that suggests she was at all involved. Plus, she was at the home with her daughter when police arrived shortly after Vickie called 911, making it practically impossible for her to have hidden the body anywhere.

Vickie had been very vocal about her belief that Mike Kearns killed her daughter, and she could be right. At the time Leigh went missing, he was living only a mile away, and police have never been able to rule him out. Considering how closely the facts of Leigh's case match the one Kearns pleaded guilty to, he is certainly a plausible suspect; police are hoping someone will finally come forward with the information they need to close the case.

Leigh Marine Occhi was just 13 years old when she went missing from Tupelo, Mississippi in August 1992. She has blue-green eyes and blonde hair, and at the time of her disappearance, she was 4 feet 10 inches tall and weighed around 95 pounds. She has a strawberry birthmark on the back of her neck. Each ear was pierced once, and she wore glasses for reading. If you have any information about Leigh's case, please call the Columbus Police Department at 614-645-4545.

Timmothy Pitzen

Timmothy Pitzen was in a great mood when his father dropped him off at kindergarten on the morning of May 11, 2011. The 6-year-old was always a ball of energy and loved being around other kids his age. He considered all the other students at his Aurora, Illinois elementary school to be his friends, and he enjoyed going to class. As Timmothy climbed out of the car, he told his father he loved him and then headed for the door of the school, swinging his Spiderman backpack from side to side. Jim Pitzen made sure his son got into the building and then drove away. He had no idea it would be the last time he would ever see Timmothy.

Amy Fry-Pitzen showed up at Timmothy's school less than an hour after her husband had dropped the boy off. She told school officials that there was a family emergency, and she needed to pick up her son. She signed him out at 8:30 am. The school's surveillance camera captured them as they went through the lobby and out the front door; Timmothy, wearing his backpack, rushed over to his mother and grabbed her hand. Nothing seemed unusual.

After leaving Timmothy's school, Amy drove 30 miles east to La Grange, Illinois. Once there, she took her Expedition to an auto repair shop and dropped it off for maintenance. Rather than sit around and wait for the work to be completed, Amy had an employee of the shop drop her and Timmothy off at the nearby Brookfield Zoo. They spent hours going through all the exhibits at the zoo, then returned to pick up the Expedition around 3:00 pm.

Jim Pitzen arrived at Timmothy's school that afternoon to pick him up and was confused when he learned Amy had signed him out that morning. He had seen his wife before she went to work that morning and everything had been normal; there was certainly no family emergency. He frantically tried to get in touch with Amy but got her voicemail. Unsure what to do, Jim went home. He kept calling Amy's phone, hoping that she would soon pull into the driveway with a good explanation.

Amy, however, had no intention of going home. From the auto repair shop, she drove 45 miles north to the Key Lime Cove Indoor Water Park and Resort in Gurnee, Illinois. She and Timmothy stayed there Wednesday night and checked out Thursday morning. Next, the pair drove 170 miles to Wisconsin Dells, Wisconsin, and checked into the Kalahari Resort for the night. They checked out the following morning at 10:10 am, and Amy finally called her mother and told her that she and Timmothy were fine. She insisted that she just needed to get away from everyone for a day or two, and would return home soon. She continued to ignore Jim's phone calls, but she did call her brother-in-law and let him talk to Timmothy so he would know the child was safe.

Amy checked into a hotel in Rockford, Illinois late Friday night, but Timmothy was not with her. The following day, hotel staff made a gruesome find in her room; Amy had killed herself. There was no sign of Timmothy, and none of his belongings were found in the room. Also missing were Amy's cell phone and the clothing she had been wearing when she picked Timmothy up from school: brown Capri pants, a white or light pink shirt, and sandals. Amy did leave a suicide note, but it only raised more questions. She wrote that Timmothy was "with people who love him and will care for him...you'll never find him."

When Jim Pitzen learned his wife had committed suicide and no one knew where Timmothy was, he was shocked. He had reported both of them missing on Thursday morning but felt better after learning that some family members had spoken to Amy. Now he struggled to comprehend what she had done.

Amy had suffered from depression in the past, but she was taking medication for it and seemed to be doing well. She had attempted suicide at least once before but had never seriously harmed herself. When she was married to her second husband she parked on some train tracks after they had an argument. She said she was going to let the train hit her, but she drove off before a train came along and checked herself into a psychiatric hospital for a week. She felt better after being placed on an antidepressant, but it wasn't enough to save the marriage.

Amy hadn't been lucky in love; Jim was her fourth husband. Timmothy was her first child, though, and she loved being a mother. Jim described her as being a wonderful mother who was completely devoted to her son, but their marriage had been rocky. Jim acknowledged that they had been arguing, especially after Amy went on a cruise without him, but they hadn't taken any steps toward divorce. Amy had been the one to mention the possibility of a separation but then seemed to back off the idea. She was terrified that she would lose custody of Timmothy if the couple did divorce; she believed a judge would give Jim custody due to her mental problems. She made it clear she was not going to allow her son to be taken away from her.

Police spoke with Jim about the possibility that Amy might have killed Timmothy before she killed herself, but he refused to believe she was capable of such an act. Her friends and family agreed with him. They all believed that, as she said in her suicide note, Amy had left Timmothy with people where he would be safe. Now they just had to find him.

Investigators were somewhat optimistic when they reviewed Amy's credit card purchases. At 11:15 am on Thursday, Amy purchased children's clothing and toys from a store in Racine, Wisconsin. None of these items had been found in the Ford or her hotel room. Also missing was Timmothy's Spiderman backpack and the booster seat he used in the car. It was possible she left these items with the people who had Timmothy.

A massive search for Timmothy was launched, with investigators from Illinois, Wisconsin, and Iowa all trying to find him. Amy's last cell phone calls on Friday had come from somewhere around Sterling, Illinois. They started the search there, plastering the area with pictures of Timmothy and making sure residents were aware of the missing child. They conducted grid searches of several areas, looking for any of Timmothy's belongings. They soon learned that Timmothy's booster seat hadn't been in the Ford when Amy drove off with him; her mother still had it from the last time she had watched Timmothy. It didn't eliminate the possibility that the boy had been left with someone, but did mean she hadn't been too concerned with his safety while driving around.

Jim and the rest of Timmothy's relatives were hopeful that he would be found quickly. If Amy really did leave him with a friend or acquaintance, there was no way they would be able to ignore all the news coverage about the child. Jim made a public plea for whoever had his son to take him to the nearest police station so he could be reunited with his family. He held his breath every time the phone rang, hoping for the news that Timmothy was coming home.

As days turned to weeks, detectives became less optimistic about Timmothy's chances of being alive. They had followed up on leads from as far away as Maine, but nothing led them to the missing child. Using Amy's cell phone records and credit card statements, they tried to reconstruct her movements to give them a better idea about where she possibly could have taken Timmothy. Hours after using her phone in Sterling, Amy stopped at a food store in Winnebago, roughly 50 miles from Sterling. Timmothy was not with her at the food store. Without knowing where Amy might have stopped in between, investigators were left with an immense area to search.

Police felt even less optimistic about Timmothy's chances of survival once forensic tests were completed on Amy's Expedition. There was a significant amount of blood in the backseat that was identified as belonging to the child. Still, his family refused to believe the worst. Timmothy had suffered from nosebleeds in the past, and investigators were unable to determine how long the blood had been there. Jim was certain the blood had come from a nosebleed a few months earlier.

The Expedition had been very dirty when it was found, and soil and vegetation samples taken from it were sent for analysis. If detectives could pinpoint exactly where the soil and plant matter was from, it would help narrow down the search area. It was determined that Amy had driven the Ford onto a gravel road or shoulder, then backed it into an open field containing plants such as black mustard and Queen Anne's lace. Detectives believe the location is most likely in northwestern Illinois.

Detectives were unable to find any connection between Amy and anyone in the Sterling area, and her friends and family didn't believe she had been there before. No one understood what would have drawn her to the area. Investigators combed through Amy's cell phone records, email account, and financial statements hoping for a clue, but found nothing. They did uncover a secret email account that no one knew she had, but computer technicians found nothing incriminating in it. Most of the 32 messages appeared to be spam.

Amy had an I-PASS account that was used to automatically pay for tolls on Illinois highways. Although the transponder was missing when police recovered her car, they were able to gain access to her account records. This allowed them to see all the tolls she had driven through, and they were shocked to discover that she had made two previous trips to the Dixon-Sterling area in the months prior to Timmothy's disappearance. She had made the drive on February 18th and again on March 20th, each time spending four to five hours in the area before getting back on the highway to head home. Her family members had been completely unaware of these trips and could think of no explanation for them. It appeared that whatever Any had done with Timmothy, it hadn't been spur of the moment. Perhaps she had arranged ahead of time to drop him off with someone in that area; perhaps she had been looking for a place to hide a body. Search teams were sent to more than two dozen sites in that area, but were unable to find anything related to the investigation.

In October 2013, a woman turned Amy's missing cell phone over to police. Incredibly, she had found it discarded on the side of a road north of Mount Carroll, Illinois, two years earlier, but never connected it to the

Pitzen case. When her brother was in need of a new cell phone, she remembered the phone she found and gave it to him to use. As soon as he charged it up and saw the names on the contact list, he recognized its importance and told his sister to contact the police. Unfortunately, the phone didn't yield any new investigative leads. Although detectives continued to follow up on every lead they received, the case slowly went cold.

The case made headlines across the nation in April 2019, when a disheveled man in Newport, Kentucky went to police and told them that he was 14-year-old Timmothy Pitzen. He claimed that he had finally escaped from the two men who had been holding him captive in an Ohio Red Roof Inn. He gave detailed descriptions of the men and their SUV, and told police where they could be found. Two Aurora detectives were sent to interview the man, but they were skeptical of his story from the beginning. He refused to allow them to take his fingerprints but did consent to a DNA test to confirm he was Timmothy. Newspapers around the country carried the story that, after eight long years, Timmothy may have been found. Unfortunately, he hadn't.

It didn't take long for detectives to confirm that the man was 23-year-old Brian Rini, a convicted felon from Medina, Ohio. His DNA was already on file due to his felony convictions, so it took less than a day to discredit his story. He had only been out of jail for a month after serving time for burglary. He told investigators that he claimed to be Timmothy because he had seen a television interview with Jim Pitzen and decided that he wanted a dad like that.

The Pitzen family was crushed. Brian didn't seem to comprehend how much pain he brought to the family, who had already been on an emotional roller coaster for years. He was charged with identity theft and making a false statement to federal authorities. Ironically, the story about his hoax was covered in more papers than the original disappearance. The increased publicity didn't bring any new leads, though, and the case soon stalled again.

Jim continues to believe Timmothy is alive somewhere, and detectives are hopeful that they will one day get the tip they need to bring some closure to the Pitzen family. The NCMEC continues to periodically produce new age progressions of Timmothy in the hopes that someone will recognize the boy and call authorities.

Timmothy Pitzen was 6 years old when he went missing in 2011. He has brown hair and brown eyes, and at the time of his disappearance he was 4 feet 2 inches tall and weighed 70 pounds. He was last seen wearing blue or green shorts, a brown t-shirt, and white socks. He was carrying a Spiderman backpack. If you have any information about Timmothy please contact the Aurora Police Department at 630-256-5000.

Peggy Rahn & Wendy Stevenson

When Wendy Stevenson woke up on the morning of December 29, 1969, she knew she was going to have a good day. Her Uncle Robert, who was visiting from Delaware, wanted to enjoy a few hours at the beach and he invited Wendy to go with him. Wendy was used to the balmy Florida winters, but Robert would soon be returning to the snow and freezing temperatures of the north. He wanted to take full advantage of the warm days before he had to leave, and his eight-year-old niece was more than happy to go with him. She changed into her blue and white bikini-style bathing suit, and then she and her older brother Danny excitedly made their way to the car.

A short distance away, nine-year-old Peggy Rahn also wanted to go to the beach. Her mother, Cecile, had to work that day – she was a single mom supporting Peggy on her own – but Peggy wasn't going to let that stop her. Robert Hedden, who rented a room in the Rahn house, had off from work that day. It didn't take much pleading on Peggy's part to get him to agree to her plan. They called Cecile to make sure she was okay with it, and then Peggy happily changed into the new, pink, baby-doll-style bikini that Santa had left under the Christmas tree for her. Minutes later, they were in the car headed to Pompano Beach.

The beach was crowded with families enjoying their holiday break and there were kids running everywhere. Peggy was an outgoing and sociable girl, and she was in her element. Robert watched in amusement as

Peggy joined the throng of kids, excitingly going from group to group, saying hello to everyone whether she knew them or not. As she made her way down closer to the water's edge, she stopped when she saw Wendy. She certainly looked familiar. The two girls actually lived quite close to each other and attended the same elementary school, but they were a year apart and didn't really know each other. At the beach, none of that mattered and the girls bonded quickly.

Although Peggy had two older sisters, Wendy only had brothers, so it was a pleasant surprise for her to have a female friend to spend the day with. The girls had quite a bit in common. Both were excellent students and well-liked by classmates and teachers alike. Though they still had a few years to go before they would be pre-teens obsessed with their appearances, both girls were starting to become interested in some of the newest fashion trends of the time. One of Peggy's sisters was a sophomore in high school, and Peggy would often emulate her in her clothing choices. From their fashionable swimsuits to the gifts that they had received for Christmas, the two girls had a lot to talk about and were happy that they had run into each other that day.

The two girls spent the morning running around the beach, splashing and playing in the sand. At one point they decided to go to the boardwalk for a while, and Robert Hedden gave each girl a quarter so they could pay the admission fee. They weren't able to get past the admission gate, however, as an employee told them they were too young to enter without adult supervision. They meandered back down the beach, probably debating if they would be able to get Robert to accompany them to the pier. But when they got back to where he had set up his beach blanket, they saw something far more exciting than walking around a boardwalk. Further down the beach, they could see a man selling ice cream and decided that would be a far better use of their quarters. They let Robert know what they were doing and ran off down the beach before he could protest. It was 1:00 pm, and it would be the last time Robert would ever see the two girls.

The beach was filled with children and adults, and there was no reason to think that the girls would get into any trouble. They had already been running around on the beach for hours without any problems. But after 15 minutes had passed, Robert was starting to get nervous. He had assumed they were going to get their ice cream and then come right back. Minutes slowly ticked by. He didn't want to overreact – it was possible the girls had run into another friend on the way and were simply standing around chatting – but after 30 minutes had gone by and he didn't see any sign of them, he began to panic.

Robert ran to the closest lifeguard and described the two girls, hoping that the lifeguard would be able to point them out in the crowd. No luck. He ran over to a different lifeguard, but he hadn't seen them either. Wendy's Uncle Robert soon joined the search. Both men knew that something was seriously wrong, and they called the police. They filed missing person reports for each girl, describing the girls and their swimsuits in great detail. That was the easy part. Their next task was far harder. They had to call each girl's mother and give them the news that would destroy their worlds. Their daughters had vanished.

News of the missing girls spread quickly on the beach, and everyone stopped what they were doing to join in the search for the two little girls. The crowd was optimistic at first. The girls had only been missing for around an hour at that point, so everyone figured that they had to be somewhere nearby.

Minutes turned into hours, and there was still no trace of Peggy or Wendy. Police knew that it was highly unlikely that the two girls had drowned; there had been multiple lifeguards on duty and the water was filled with people. Surely someone would have noticed if the girls had been struggling in the water. High tide had been around noon, but it was a calm day and the water was clear. No one wanted to say the words out loud, but if they hadn't wandered away and they hadn't drowned, it left only one horrible alternative: abduction. Was it possible that someone had managed to abduct two young girls from a crowded beach without anyone seeing a thing? Lifeguards estimated that there had been a total of 4400 people on the beach at 1:00 pm.

The mothers of the girls were torn. Wendy's mom had taught Wendy from an early age that she was never to go anywhere with a stranger. She couldn't imagine that her daughter would have willingly gotten into a car with anyone, and for that reason, she could almost believe that the girls had drowned. Peggy's mom did believe that the girls had been abducted. Peggy was far too strong a swimmer to have drowned, and she was sure that drowning would have attracted attention. She feared that someone had managed to lure the girls off the beach and away from the crowds before forcing them into a vehicle. The investigators made it clear that they were keeping an open mind, but they appeared to be learning towards the abduction theory as well. They appealed to the public for help, hoping that someone out there had seen something out of the ordinary that would help lead them to the two girls.

The entire community united to try to find Peggy and Wendy. People postponed their New Year's celebrations that weekend so they could join in the search. Over 300 volunteers gathered to comb through the beach and surrounding areas. In 1969, parts of Broward County were still untouched by development, leaving many sparsely populated areas that needed to be searched. In addition to beaches and the ocean, the county also contained wooded areas, swamps, canals, and rock pits. Many of the areas were searched on foot, with people standing elbow to elbow to ensure that nothing was missed. Other search parties went out on horseback and motorcycles, while dune buggies and boats scoured the coastal areas. Helicopters flew over the entire search area, hoping to spot something from the air that had been missed by those on the ground. Although police didn't think the girls would be found in the water, dive teams were sent in anyway just to be sure. It was a massive search effort, and the disappearance of the girls made headlines around the country.

The high publicity that the case received led to a large number of possible tips being called in. Detectives sorted through thousands of phone messages, painstakingly following up on each lead. One of the first calls they received was from Betty Fischer, a clerk at a convenience store not too far from the beach. She had been working a night shift that Monday when the girls went missing, and sometime around midnight a male customer entered the store with two young girls. He had purchased cigarettes for himself and ice cream for the two girls. It seemed to be a routine transaction, and the girls hadn't seemed to be at all nervous. The only reason Betty remembered them at all was because the girls had both been clad only in bathing suits despite the fact that the night air was quite chilly.

The next morning, Betty heard someone mention

that two girls had gone missing the previous day and she immediately called the police to report what she had seen. An officer was sent over with pictures to see if Betty would be able to identify the girls that she had seen. When she realized that she had indeed seen the two girls that were missing, she immediately burst into tears. There was no way she could have known, and the girls had seemed to be perfectly calm, but she was inconsolable. If only she had known sooner, she never would have let them leave the store. All she could do now was give the police a description of the man the girls had been seen with and hope that it would help detectives find the two girls.

Betty said the girls had been with a white male, around 25-30 years old, with sandy hair and blue-gray eyes. He was about six feet tall and weighed approximately 200 pounds, and she had noticed that he had a two-inch scar running along the back of his right hand between his thumb and forefinger. He and the girls had driven off in a 1966 or 1967 metallic blue Chevrolet with a black top and wire wheel covers.

Betty gave police so many details that they believed she was embellishing, perhaps to alleviate the guilt she felt for not realizing the girls had been abducted. The detectives actually asked her if she would be willing to take a lie detector test, and she agreed. The test results indicated that she was telling the truth, but police still seemed uncertain as to whether or not the girls she had seen were actually Peggy and Wendy. They had gone missing around 1:00 pm. It seemed unlikely that someone who abducted them would be bold enough to remain in the same area with them almost 12 hours later, but they also knew criminals could be not counted on to behave in rational ways.

Three days after the girls went missing, detectives

got a call from the manager of a camera store in Riviera Beach, located about 40 miles away from Pompano Beach. Employees there believed that the two girls had come into the store by themselves to inquire about getting a camera repaired. They asked what the cost would be, and then left the store after telling the employees that they would be back. They never returned. Though the employees were certain they had seen Peggy and Wendy, it seems unlikely.

Another potential sighting came from a police chief in Georgia, who claimed he had been at a convenience store and had seen the two girls sitting in a car with Florida license plates. He spoke with them briefly and they said that they were going on vacation with their cousin. Pointing out the dresses they were wearing, they said that their cousin had even bought them new clothes for the trip. There was a man using a payphone in the parking lot, and the chief assumed that this was the cousin they were talking about. News of the missing girls hadn't made it up the Georgia coast at that time, and the police chief said that it wasn't until after he saw a teletype on Peggy and Wendy that he realized they matched the descriptions of the missing girls. He wasn't able to give a good description of the male they were with, so it's unclear if he saw the same man that Betty Fisher reported seeing, and there is no way to confirm that the two girls really were Wendy and Peggy. The man on the payphone didn't seem at all concerned when he looked over and saw a police officer talking to the two girls. If it had been Wendy and Peggy, it's hard to believe that, given the opportunity to have an unsupervised conversation with a uniformed police officer, they would have chosen to volunteer information about their new clothes and their vacation plans and not the fact that they had been taken against their will. Although detectives weren't quite sure just how credible of a lead it was, the police chief had made the drive to Florida to speak with them, and it was obvious that he truly believed he had seen Wendy and Peggy. The detectives working the case knew that they could use this lead to their advantage. If the girls had been seen in Georgia, it meant that state lines had been crossed, and that one fact would be enough to trigger FBI involvement in the case.

After a psychic told Peggy's mother that he believed the girls had drowned, rumors quickly began spreading that the girls' bodies were going to be found in the ocean. Police still did not believe that the girls had drowned, but admitted that there was a remote possibility that they could have fallen in and gotten trapped in a seawall that had been built to help prevent beach erosion. Construction had been done on the seawall around the time that the girls went missing, so the construction company agreed to tear down the 25-foot section of the seawall where the girls may have ended up. The area was then thoroughly searched, but there was no evidence of the girls at all.

The investigators were kept busy following up on leads that were coming in from all over the country, but nothing seemed to be bringing them closer to finding the two girls. For many of the officers, this case was personal. Most of them were fathers. All of them wanted to be able to find the girls and bring them home safely. They couldn't just wait idly for leads to be called in. They looked into every sex offender who lived in the area. They interviewed all of them at least once. But they also knew that many of the people who had been on the beach the day the girls went missing had been from out of town. It was one of the main drawbacks of working in a town that catered to tourists.

As in all missing children cases, the parents of the

girls would also be thoroughly investigated. Both girls had divorced parents that didn't necessarily get along with each other. Detectives considered the possibility that the disappearances had been part of a twisted custody battle, but the fact that both girls had gone missing made this seem unlikely. A parent probably would have targeted only their own child.

Peggy's mother didn't believe that her ex-husband had anything to do with it, but she was terrified by the thought Robert Hedden might have been involved. He had never given her any reason not to trust him, but she found herself second-guessing everything and wondered if she had put her daughter in danger by allowing him to take her to the beach. She went into the room that he rented off of her, took the clothes that he had worn to the beach, and handed them over to police for testing. Robert cooperated fully with the investigators, and he agreed to take a polygraph examination. He passed it with no problems and was ruled out as a possible suspect.

Slowly, the police were able to rule many people out as suspects, but they weren't any closer to finding the person responsible for the girls' disappearance and the entire town was on edge. Like most of the coastal towns in Florida, Pompano Beach had a steady stream of tourists; they were critical to the economic livelihood of the town. While residents certainly welcomed the tourist dollars that were spent in their town, they were wary of strangers. In April, a man was using a payphone inside one of the restaurants downtown. A couple of the employees and customers noticed that he had left an open notebook at the counter where he had been sitting, and they could clearly see "Rahn" and "Stevenson" written on the top of the page. Suspicious that the man had something to do with the missing girls, they immediately called the police.

The man left the restaurant as a police car pulled up. The responding officer questioned the man but felt that he was being evasive in his answers and that the man had been trying to get away from him. The man said he had been finished with his phone call and hadn't even seen the police car when he was leaving.

Not satisfied with the man's responses, the officer arrested him for disorderly conduct, an obvious excuse to take the man into custody so they could find out just what he knew about the two missing girls. It turned out that the man actually knew quite a bit about Peggy and Wendy, but not because he had anything to do with their disappearance. He was a reporter from *"Today"* who was covering the story about the missing girls. The booking process was quickly stopped, and an embarrassed Lt. Kennedy, the detective in charge of the case, granted the reporter an interview. He apologized for what had happened, noting that everyone was still edgy about the missing girls and had a tendency of jumping at shadows.

For the entire first year that her daughter was missing, Cecile Rahn stopped at the police station every single morning when she was on her way to work. She always got the same heartbreaking response. Eventually, her brother-in-law began going in her place. It was simply too hard for her as the months went by with no movement on the case. She was convinced that the girls were alive but was worried that they had amnesia and weren't able to remember who they were or where they lived. She held on to a pair of Peggy's favorite pajamas long after her daughter would have outgrown them, hoping that Peggy would be found and the pajamas would trigger her memory to return.

Despite the long hours that detectives put into the case, eventually they were forced to admit that the case was beginning to go cold. They had chased down leads in numerous states and followed up on hundreds of potential sightings, but were unable to uncover any tangible evidence of what had happened to the two girls after they left the beach. Soon, five years had gone by. For some, the memory of the tragedy had faded with time, but for the families of the girls – and the detectives who had tried so desperately to find them – no amount of time could lessen the pain.

Two detectives were still assigned to follow up on the occasional leads that were still called in, but they admitted that they were no closer to determining where the girls were than they had been on the first day they went missing. There had been over 2,000 reported sightings of the girls, called in from almost every state in the country. None of them got detectives any closer to the girls.

By 1974, the girls would have reached their teenage years if they were still alive. Peggy's mother still clung to the hope that her daughter was out there. She lived in the same house and had the same phone number, convinced that one day Peggy would contact her. She still left a kitchen light on all night just in case. Wendy's family had moved away from the area, the pain too much for them to bear. They knew that the girls were most likely not alive, but couldn't give up on a small spark of hope that a miracle would happen. Unfortunately, the miracle never came.

It's been more than 50 years since Wendy and Peggy went strolling down a beach to get ice cream, and then vanished into thin air. Despite the reported sightings of the pair, police were never able to confirm any of them. Exactly what happened to the girls is still a mystery, but there are several possible theories. Did they simply wander off and get lost? Did someone abduct them from the beach? Could they have drowned?

There are some who believe that Peggy and Wendy were victims of Gerald Schaefer, who was convicted of killing two teenage girls in 1973. Police suspect there were far more victims that he was never prosecuted for, and Schaefer himself bragged that he had killed at least 80 people.

Schaefer's family had moved to Fort Lauderdale when he was a teenager, and he graduated from high school there in 1964. He later claimed that he knew he was a sexual deviant from the time he was a young boy, and said that he began seeing a psychiatrist in 1966, seeking relief from the sexual and homicidal fantasies that were taking over his life. If he did indeed seek treatment, it didn't help.

He decided that he wanted to become a priest, but was turned away from the seminary for not having enough faith. He then tried to become a teacher, but he was kicked out of two different student teaching programs for trying to impose his rigid moral and political values on his students. He did manage to get married in 1968, but his wife left him in 1970, citing extreme cruelty. He rebounded quickly and decided to become a police officer. He tried to get a job with the Broward County Sheriff's Department, but they rejected him when he was unable to pass the required psychological exam.

Eventually, he was able to obtain a job with the Wilton Manors police department, a small unit in Fort Lauderdale. He didn't last long there. He was fired in April of 1972. The FBI would later say that he was fired for repeatedly pulling over females under the pretense of a traffic violation just so he could run their information through the police department computer. Once he had their personal information, he would call them and harass them to go out with him.

By June of 1972, he had moved to Stuart, Florida, and obtained a job with the Martin County Sheriff's Office. He didn't even last an entire month. In July, he picked up two female teenagers who had been hitchhiking. After lying to them and telling them that hitchhiking was illegal in Martin County, he pretended to cut them a break – as long as they agreed to meet up with him the next day to go to the beach. It was a mistake that the girls would quickly regret. Instead of driving them to the beach, he drove them to a swampy area and began making sexual remarks to them. He forced them out of the car at gunpoint and tied them to trees with nooses around their necks. He told them he intended to sell them into sexual slavery, but he had some work he needed to take care of first. He left the two terrified teens precariously balancing on tree roots, knowing that if they slipped, they would hang themselves. The teenagers were not going to stick around to find out what he intended to do; shortly after he left, they managed to free themselves. Hysterical, they made it to a nearby highway and were able to flag down a passing police car. When Schaefer returned to the scene, he seemed genuinely dumbfounded that the two girls had managed to escape in his absence. He was in trouble, and he knew it. He had been overconfident and cocky in his ability to control the women, and because of that, he had told them his real name. He tried to come up with a quick cover story, calling the sheriff and telling him that he had "overdone" his job. He insisted that he had simply wanted to scare the two girls so that they wouldn't hitchhike anymore. It was a move that cost him both his job and his freedom. He pleaded guilty to assault and the false imprisonment charge was dropped.

On January 15, 1973, the former cop became a prison inmate. Unfortunately, it was too late. As police would soon learn, when Schaefer had been out on bond in September of 1972, he murdered two teenagers. Their remains were found that March. They had been tied to trees and then butchered. Eyewitness accounts and evidence obtained from Schaefer's home proved that he had been the killer. While he would only ever go on trial for that killing, police suspected that he had committed many other murders, a claim that Schaefer was more than happy to admit to. He was later killed in prison by another inmate, and the total death count may never be known. Was it possible that he had abducted and killed Peggy and Wendy?

There is no doubt that Schaefer terrorized women throughout southern Florida. When his home was searched, investigators found women's jewelry and newspaper clippings about various missing women, including two women that had gone missing in 1969. Investigators also found identification from two females who had gone missing in January of 1973, about a week before Schaefer began his prison sentence. Their bodies weren't found until 1977, but any evidence that may have pointed to their killer had deteriorated by that point and Schaefer was never charged with their murders.

There was speculation that Schaefer had been involved in the disappearances of dozens of women, but they were all teenagers. Some believed that Peggy and Wendy had been too young to have been victims of Schaefer, but that alone isn't enough to exonerate him. While most serial killers do stick to a specific victim profile, many of them are also opportunistic. Ted Bundy preferred college women, but that didn't stop him from abducting and killing a 12-year-old girl who had the misfortune of crossing his path.

Schaefer was in the area when Peggy and Wendy went missing, and it's very possible he did see them at the beach and somehow manage to lure them into getting into a car with him. Although he bragged about the number of murders he had committed, Schaefer never directly admitted to law enforcement that he had killed the two little girls. He did, however, tell a friend that he had killed them after reading a comment from serial killer Albert Fish, who was alleged to have killed and eaten several children and who had made crude remarks about how delicious young children were. Schaefer wrote in a letter to his girlfriend that "Peggy and Wendy just happened along at a time when I was curious about Fish's cravings for the flesh of young girls...I assure you these girls were not molested sexually. I found both of them very satisfactory, particularly sautéed with onions and peppers."

Schaefer would later estimate the number of women that he killed to be somewhere around 80-110, a truly outlandish figure. Like most killers, it's highly likely that he was taking credit for a number of murders that he didn't actually have anything to do with, but he wanted the notoriety that was associated with such a large body count. Investigators who searched Schaefer's room found a large number of souvenirs he had kept from women he had killed as well as newspaper clippings on many women who were still missing. They didn't find anything belonging to Wendy or Peggy, nor were there any clippings about their disappearance. It's certainly possible that Schaefer broke from his normal pattern and abducted the two little girls, but it's not a foregone conclusion and the real killer of Wendy and Peggy may still be out there somewhere.

It's possible that the girls, deep in conversation

about their Christmas gifts, fashion, or some other topic, wandered much further along the beach than they had intended and ended up in an isolated area where they didn't have the safety of a crowd to protect them. If that had happened, they would have been extremely vulnerable. Although they had both been taught to never go anywhere with a stranger, if they had gotten lost on the beach or in the woods that surrounded the area, it's possible that they would have accepted a stranger's offer to help them.

At the time the girls went missing, Pompano Beach was making a name for itself as a tourist destination, but it was still a fairly small town with many rural, isolated spaces. Could the girls have wandered off and gotten so lost that no one could find them? There were certainly many wooded and swampy areas, but none right along the beach. It's unlikely that the girls could have walked so far that they ended up outside of the area that search parties went through. The construction boom that took place in the years after the girls went missing turned most of the remote and undeveloped areas into subdivisions and shopping centers. It's reasonable to assume that the girls' bodies would have been found by construction crews at some point, but no trace of them was ever unearthed.

Early on in the investigation, detectives believed there was some possibility that the girls had drowned, but this doesn't seem like a probable scenario. It's not unheard of for people to drown after being caught in a swift undertow, and some bodies that are swept out to sea are never recovered. But the waters were calm on the day the girls went missing, and there were so many people around that the idea of the two girls both becoming overwhelmed by the water without anyone seeing it is improbable.

Exactly what happened to Wendy and Peggy is as much a mystery today as it was in 1969. They remain listed as missing persons; the investigation is still open and the case remains unsolved.

Peggy Rahn was just 9 years old when she went missing from Pompano Beach, Florida in December 1969. She had blue eyes and blonde hair, and at the time of her disappearance, she was 4 feet 4 inches tall and weighed 67 pounds. She was last seen wearing a pink baby-doll-style bathing suit with fringe.

Wendy Stevenson was just 8 years old when she went missing along with Peggy. Wendy had hazel eyes and brown hair, and at the time of her disappearance, she was 4 feet 2 inches tall and weighed 61 pounds. She was last seen wearing a blue and white checkered bikini. If you have any information about Peggy and Wendy, please contact the Broward County Sheriff's Office at 954-493-8477.

Kemberly Ramer

Kemberly Ramer was having a great time on Friday, August 15, 1997. The 17-year-old played in a softball game and then went out with some friends. She ended her night with a visit to her boyfriend, and neighbors saw her car pull into her driveway a few minutes before her midnight curfew. Kem's parents were divorced, and she lived with her father in Opp, Alabama. On this evening, she had the house to herself, as her father was staying overnight with his girlfriend. She kicked off her shoes as soon as she got into her bedroom and then got ready for bed. She had to be up early the next morning to stop by the high school; they would be assigning parking spaces for the upcoming school year. She was scheduled to start her senior year at Opp High School in just a few days, and she was very excited.

Kenneth Ramer arrived home early Saturday morning and found the house empty. He wasn't particularly concerned, as Kem would sometimes go shopping with her mother on weekends. Sue Ramer lived about 10 miles away, just over the Florida border, and he assumed she had picked Kem up that morning. When Kem still wasn't home the next day, he called his ex-wife to see if she knew when Kem would be returning. He was startled to learn that Sue hadn't heard from Kem all weekend. They quickly began calling all of Kem's friends and realized that no one had seen her since Friday night. Panicking, Kenneth called the Opp Police Department and reported his daughter missing.

The first 48 hours are critical in any missing person case, and police had already lost most of that window. By the time police got involved, Kem hadn't been seen for more than 36 hours. Detectives tried to piece together what she had done in the hours before she went missing. They determined that she had returned home from her boyfriend's house around midnight, and it was clear she made it inside the house. Her car was in the driveway, and her keys were found in her bedroom. Looking around her room, it appeared that some kind of struggle had taken place. Her bed sheets were messed up as if she had gotten into bed, but her pillow was on the floor and a picture had fallen off the wall.

Police were certain that Kem had not left on her own. All of her belongings, including her purse, glasses, keys, and money were still in her bedroom, and none of her shoes were missing. Wherever she was, she was barefoot. That fact, along with the evidence of a struggle, led police to conclude that Kem had most likely been abducted from her bedroom at some point after midnight but before 6:00 am.

Kem was a friendly and outgoing girl who got straight As in school and had no known enemies. She was a cheerleader and played second base on the school's softball team, and planned to go to the University of South Alabama and major in physical therapy after graduating from high school. She had gotten her senior pictures taken just a few days before she disappeared and had been looking forward to her senior year of high school. Detectives interviewed her friends and her boyfriend, and all of them described her as very happy with her life. She was not the sort of teenager who would run away from home; she was very close with her family and had no personal problems.

Opp, Alabama was a tiny town of 6900 residents, and it was considered an extremely safe place for families. Violent crime was essentially unheard of, and people rarely locked their doors. Kem's disappearance shook the entire community and shattered their illusion of safety. The Opp Police Department knew right away that they weren't equipped to handle the case on their own, and immediately called the FBI for assistance.

Local searches for Kem turned up no leads, and police were able to eliminate her parents, other family members, and her boyfriend as suspects. Although they released very little information about the case, they did say that several phone calls had been placed from Kem's house to a number in Florida around the time they believe Kem was abducted. They did not believe it was a number that Kem would have been familiar with, leading them to conclude that it was most likely the abductor who called the number. Despite making several attempts, the caller was unable to reach anyone at the number called, and police did not say who the number was registered to. Because the number was located in Florida, however, they said it was very possible that Kem had been taken across state lines. They searched in multiple locations in both Alabama and Florida but came up empty each time.

Search planes flew over the area, volunteers covered miles of terrain, family and friends posted thousands of missing person posters throughout the county, and detectives interviewed anyone who had come in contact with Kem. Truck drivers picked up hundreds of missing person flyers and hung them up all over the country. Nothing led to Kem.

Kem's friends had to start the school year without her, and they were fearful for their own safety. The person responsible for Kem's abduction was still out there somewhere, and everyone worried that they could be the next target. Police did what they could to reassure the public that they were working to get the case resolved, but it did little to calm the fear that was running through the community. They collected money and offered a reward for information in the case, holding onto the hope that Kem was still alive and they might be able to bring her home.

In December 1997, Kenneth and Sue Ramer held a press conference to remind the public that Kem was still missing. They begged for help in finding their daughter, urging anyone with any information to contact police. They were certain that someone out there had the information they needed.

Months went by, and the investigation seemed to be at a standstill. Police followed up on every lead that was called in, but they were unable to develop a solid theory about what had happened to Kem that night. On May 18, 1998, the day when Kem should have been celebrating her 18th birthday, the FBI began investigating a pond known as Steep Hole in Leonia, Florida. They had received a tip that Kem's body had been placed into the Walton County pond, which was owned by a logging company. Although the pond was in a gated area and had "no trespassing" signs posted around it, the gate had not been locked during the time Kem disappeared, and the numerous beer bottles found in the area seemed to indicate that it was often used as a party spot. It was located about 10 miles away from the Alabama state line, and 30 miles away from Kem's Opp home.

The FBI felt that the Steep Hole tip was their most credible one yet and sent in a team of cadaver dogs to search the area. When they appeared to pick up on the scent of human remains, the FBI sent in a team of divers to explore the water. The divers were hindered by tannic acid in the water; the black water made it nearly impossible to see and they had to feel their way around. They used metal detectors, hoping to find traces of the gold bracelet and anklet Kem had been wearing when she vanished. When that failed, they had lighting equipment brought in to help increase the visibility in the pond. They spent three days searching through the water basin, which reached depths of 35 feet. They found nothing to indicate that Kem had ever been there.

Over the years, the FBI and local police would conduct hundreds of searches for Kem, both on land and in water. Her mother also continued to search, spending every weekend going through different wooded areas looking for her daughter. Although tips continued to trickle in, nothing brought police any closer to locating Kemberly.

In July 2006, a sinkhole near Ponce de Leon, Florida was searched after the FBI received an anonymous tip claiming that Kem had fallen into the water there. The hole was 55 feet deep and 300 feet across, and the FBI sent a team of 10 divers to investigate the claim. They believed the tip was credible because the phone number that had been dialed from Kem's house the night she disappeared had been located in the Ponce de Leon area, though they were never able to connect it to the case. Still, divers spent a total of 35 hours in the water, hoping to find something. They were unsuccessful.

The search of the sinkhole failed to yield any evidence, but the resulting publicity did prompt a few new tips to be forwarded to the FBI. Several people called with information that was new to investigators, and they followed up on all leads, hoping they were getting closer to unraveling the mystery of what happened to Kem. They continued interviewing people and searched several more areas in Florida, but answers remained elusive.

In 2015, police received a detailed tip stating that Kem's body would be found in an area behind an abandoned house in Coffee County, and a search team was sent to check into the lead. The house, located off County Road 412 near the Covington County line, was falling apart. Investigators concentrated on what had been an old well behind the property, bringing in a backhoe and digging down more than 30 feet into the ground. They found nothing that suggested Kem had been there.

In 2019, police put together an updated flyer about Kem's case and posted it throughout the area. They were hoping this would remind the public about the case and bring in some new leads. Both local police and the FBI continue to actively investigate Kem's disappearance. Over the years they have conducted thousands of interviews, but still need critical information to solve the case. They do have a couple of suspects in the case, but they have not released any names and do not have enough information to charge anyone.

There have been rumors for years that one of the suspects was the son of a Walton County sheriff's deputy who was dating a member of Kem's family at the time she disappeared, but this has not been confirmed. One deputy alleged he was fired for trying to look into the connection between Kem and the deputy's son, but this was never substantiated in court. The Walton County Sheriff's Office is not one of the lead investigating agencies on the case, and it is unlikely they would be able to hinder the FBI's investigation into one of their own. The FBI will not comment publicly on potential suspects but has said that they are confident there are still people living in the Opp area who know what happened to Kem and they hope they will come forward with this information.

Kemberly Ramer was just 17 years old when she went missing from Opp, Alabama in August 1997. She has brown hair and brown eyes, and at the time of her disappearance, she was 5 feet 4 inches tall and weighed approximately 130 pounds. She was last seen wearing a white t-shirt with brightly colored designs on the front and cut-off gray sweatpants. She had clear braces on her teeth and was also wearing a gold bracelet, necklace, and anklet. If you have any information about Kemberly, please call the Opp Police Department at 334-493-4511 or the FBI at 202-324-3000.

Jonathan Schaff

It was a cold night in Granville, New York – the temperature would bottom out at 21 degrees – but it was warm inside the Riverside Pub. The pub, situated on Main Street, was less than a mile away from the New York/Vermont border. It was common for people from Vermont to patronize the bar, likely due to the fact that they could drink longer there. Last call in Vermont was 2:00 am, while it was 4:00 am in New York. The bar was crowded with people taking advantage of this in the early morning hours of January 18, 2014.

Jonathan Schaff, a 23-year-old who lived in Fair Haven, Vermont, was one of the patrons at the Riverside that night. His father, John Schaff, was there as well. Jonathan spent a few hours at the bar socializing with friends as well as his father and was in no hurry to leave. When John told his son he was heading home, Jonathan said he was going to stay because he was having a great time. John left around 3:00 am to return to his home in Cambridge, New York. Father and son exchanged quick goodbyes, and John told Jonathan to give him a call if he needed anything. He had no idea it would be the last time he would see his son.

Not long after John left, a disagreement of some kind took place between Jonathan and another man. It's unclear exactly what started the argument, but it ended in a fistfight that was quickly broken up by some of the other patrons. Neither of the two men involved in the fight was seriously injured, although Jonathan was hit hard enough to break his glasses. According to witnesses, he sustained a couple of cuts on his face from his broken glasses, but he appeared fine otherwise.

Once the fight was over, the bar settled down. Cops would later categorize the fight as "a misunderstanding" between two intoxicated individuals. Neither man left the bar right away, and there didn't appear to be any hard feelings between them. Jonathan remained at the bar until last call, and he left around 4:30 am. He walked out with a 33-year-old female and a 26-year-old male, both from the Fair Haven area. He had just met them that evening, and they had offered to give him a ride home.

The couple had parked their car in the Loomis Trucking Company parking lot, which was located right over the state line in Vermont. It was just a short walk down Route 149, which was known as Main Street in Granville. It was quite common for people heading to the bar to park across the state line in Vermont; Granville had its own police force, and they were more likely to get pulled over for DUI on the New York side of the border. That area of Vermont was more rural and less frequently patrolled. In addition, as you cross into New York on Route 149, there is a sign reminding people that there is a winter parking ban in effect in Granville. "No parking on village streets, November 1 to April 1, from 11:00 pm to 5:00 am." With limited parking options, it made sense to park in Vermont and walk across the border.

Walking on Route 149 from the Riverside Pub would have taken the trio through a residential area, with modest homes on both sides of the street. Route 149 is not a large highway, just a two-lane road with a shoulder on each side. The stretch of road running from the pub to the trucking company is flat but somewhat curvy. Heading towards Vermont, there is a sidewalk on the left side of the street until the state line was crossed. Once in Vermont, the sidewalk ends, and the shoulders get narrower. By the time you reach Loomis Trucking Company, there is no shoulder at all, so they would have been walking in the street.

Jonathan left the bar with the couple, but it isn't clear if he accepted their offer to drive him home or not. Either way, he was walking down Highway 149 with them, but when they stopped briefly to light cigarettes, he continued walking and they lost sight of him around a curve. When they got to the parking lot, he was nowhere to be seen. Assuming he had gotten another ride home, the couple left. Jonathan never made it home and was never seen again.

Jonathan lived with his mother, May Winchell, at the time he went missing. She started to get worried when he never returned from his night out, and when he didn't show up for his scheduled shift at Walmart that afternoon, she reported him missing.

The investigation was complicated by the fact that no one could say exactly where Jonathan disappeared, making it hard to determine which police force would have jurisdiction over the case. Officers from the Granville Police Department were the first to respond to the missing person call since Jonathan left the Riverside Pub shortly before vanishing; that seemed the best place to begin the investigation.

After interviewing several people who had been at the bar the night before, police learned about the bar fight that had taken place, but didn't believe it had anything to do with Jonathan's subsequent disappearance. Witnesses said that the fight hadn't been serious, and there were no major injuries. After the altercation, Jonathan had a few cuts on the bridge of his nose, but that was about it. According to Granville Police Chief Ernest Bassett, "From all reports, it was nothing too serious. Once it was over, it was over." Both parties involved remained at the bar and there was no further trouble between the two of them.

Chief Bassett spoke with the two people who had left the bar with Jonathan, and they explained that they had lost track of him at some point along the way to the parking lot. "When the two who were with him got to their car, he wasn't there." They were questioned extensively, but police said there was no reason to believe they had anything to do with the disappearance.

No one could say for certain if he made it to the parking lot or not, but he had definitely been headed in that direction. Chief Bassett was concerned, because the Mettawee River was extremely close to Loomis Trucking, with some of their trailers parked within 40 feet of the water. There was a steep, 10-foot embankment that dropped down to the river at the back of the parking lot. If Jonathan had gotten too close to the water and fallen in, he may have been too intoxicated to get himself back out.

Searches were taking place in both New York and Vermont, as investigators worked to establish the last confirmed location of Jonathan. The two people who had been walking with him believed that he had made it over the state line into Vermont; a command post was set up in the town of Wells, Vermont, only minutes away from Granville. Vermont State Police, New York State Police, and Granville Police would all be taking part in the search.

According to Vermont State Police Capt. Donald Patch, they were investigating the case from all angles and had not yet ruled anything out. Searchers were focusing on all routes Jonathan could have taken from Route 149. His cell phone records indicated that he may have been somewhere in the vicinity of Sheldon's Concrete or the Newmont Slate Company, both on Route 149 in Pawlet, or off of Bullfrog Hollow Road in the same general area. There had been no activity on his cell phone since around the time he went missing, and with no idea of which direction he had gone in, they were unable to narrow the search for him. Capt. Patch was blunt; they had no idea what had happened to Jonathan. "Our evidence is he didn't show up at work and he didn't return home. We're hoping someone will come forward with some information."

The weather wasn't helping the search effort. The area had gotten a couple of inches of snow between the time Jonathan was last seen and the time he was reported missing, and up to five more inches were expected to fall on Monday. While the police dogs were still able to track in the snow, it hindered the human cops because it could cover up any footprints, items, or other evidence that could be related to the case.

On Tuesday, they got their first bit of evidence: Jonathan's cell phone was found. It had been in the cab of an abandoned truck in the Loomis Trucking parking lot. There were a lot of unused trailers and trucks on the property, and the one his phone was in had not been moved for a while. They couldn't know for sure if Jonathan had left his phone there or if someone else had, but they were working under the assumption it had been him. This meant that he had last been seen in Vermont, and the Vermont State Police would be the lead agency on the case. The Granville Police and the New York State Police would continue to assist in the investigation, though, and searches would take place in both states.

The weather cleared up enough on Tuesday that helicopters were no longer grounded, and an Army

National Guard helicopter was used to conduct aerial searches of the roads, fields, and rivers in the area. They were unable to find any relevant evidence but would continue to conduct sporadic searches over the next few months.

Wednesday was a rough day for Jonathan's family and friends, as it was his 24th birthday. Many left messages on his Facebook wall, wishing him a happy birthday and praying he would be home soon. Many still hadn't been able to fully process the fact that he was missing.

Since Jonathan's phone had been found so close to the Mettawee River, investigators spent a lot of time concentrating on the area of the river that flowed directly behind Loomis Trucking. The river had been running unusually fast at the time Jonathan went missing, making it even more dangerous if he had fallen in while intoxicated. The Vermont State Police brought in their dive team to check the river, but they were only able to do a limited search due to the extremely cold weather and the fast-flowing river. There was a deep pool in the river behind the parking lot that police had hoped to send divers into, but the weather simply wasn't cooperating.

The land search for Jonathan was expanded, and searchers covered all possible roads he could have taken from the area around the parking lot. Teams searched five or six miles in each direction, looking for anything that could help them pinpoint where Jonathan could be. Police also asked people who lived in the area to walk their property and check for anything out of the ordinary. Residents carefully went through their land, checking sheds, outbuildings, and vehicles in case Jonathan had tried to seek shelter out of the elements. Unfortunately, no one was able to find anything that was suspicious or out of place.

Temperatures in the area were dropping below zero in the overnight hours, and this cold weather was a huge concern. No one could survive very long under those conditions. Capt. Patch noted that they still had no conclusive evidence showing that Jonathan wasn't alive. "We're going to continue searching for him. Until we know otherwise, we have to assume that he's alive. We're obviously concerned about the temperatures in the subzero range." It was a concern for Jonathan's family and friends as well. They pleaded for anyone with information to please come forward.

Investigators were interested in speaking with anyone who had any contact with Jonathan around the time that he had gone missing. They wanted to put together a complete timeline of events that went on before he went missing as well as after. They had interviewed many of the people who had been at the Riverside Pub with Jonathan, and they would re-interview a number of them. Capt. Patch had hoped to get useful information from Jonathan's cell phone, but they found nothing at all relevant to the disappearance. "The case is still evolving. We're just going to keep working it and using all the resources that we have."

Kenneth Winning, Jonathan's best friend, was convinced that something terrible had happened to him. He said Jonathan had been his best friend since fifth grade, and there was no way Jonathan would have walked away from his life. There was no way he was missing by choice. Kenneth was upset with how the newspapers kept playing up the fact that there had been a fight at the pub before Jonathan went missing, and was disappointed with how the articles seemed to portray Jonathan as some kind of thug. "He was a pretty quiet kid. He wouldn't hurt anybody. Unless someone attacked him or was hurting a girl, then I could see it."

Kenneth last spoke to his best friend on Friday evening. Jonathan had called him to see if he wanted to get together that night. Kenneth, a truck driver, was unable to go out that night because he was out of the state, returning from Ohio. He couldn't understand how Jonathan could simply disappear without a trace. "I think people know more. Somebody knows more than what's being said. He's just not the kind of kid who walks off into the wilderness and vanishes."

May Winchell was also trying to figure out how her son could have vanished without a trace. She was upset by the focus on the river because she refused to entertain the thought that Jonathan could have drowned. "I think Jonathan is still out there, and alive...I want him to come home." May and Jonathan had a special bond. He was her youngest child, her baby. Normally, he would call her for a ride if he had been drinking at a bar or a friend's house. It made no sense to her that he would have a ride from two people he didn't even know. It was completely out of character for him. "I wish he had called me. None of this would have happened."

A week after the search for Jonathan began, police still had no idea what had happened to him. Except for his cell phone, they hadn't been able to locate anything to give them a clue about where the missing man had gone. Many of the officers involved in the case believed Jonathan had ended up in the Mettawee River, but the weather conditions needed to improve before divers would be able to search for him there. Vermont State Police Detective Lt. Kevin Lane told reporters that the divers would have to wait until their commander determined that both water and weather conditions were deemed safe; current conditions were simply too risky.

"It's been bitterly cold. I don't know if it's been above 10 degrees, and then you add the wind chill onto that... [the divers] start having equipment failures if they're too cold." None of the officers wanted to wait, they all wanted to be able to bring closure to the case. It was hard on the whole team, and even harder on Jonathan's family.

Detective Lt. Lane stated that they still had no evidence that foul play had taken place, but they were still very worried about Jonathan's safety. "It's just highly unusual that he'd be gone for this amount of time. It's not something he'd typically do or had done in the past. He lived with his mother and they had a good relationship." They didn't think it at all likely that Jonathan had voluntarily left on his own, but they knew that the alternative was far worse.

On January 30th, the Vermont State Police SCUBA team and a police dog team conducted an extensive search of the Mettawee River and its banks. While the divers were unable to enter the water due to the weather, they used an underwater camera to see if they could locate anything. They covered a stretch of the river near Loomis Trucking but found nothing.

It wasn't until February 28th that dive teams were able to fully search the Mettawee River. Representatives from agencies in both New York and Vermont worked together to coordinate the search. They were focusing on an area of the river that was adjacent to the parking lot where Jonathan's cell phone had been found. Search dogs were brought through the area on several occasions and showed interest in a certain spot multiple times. Police brought in a backhoe so they could break through some of the ice on the river, but found mostly logs and debris. Still, they went through the site thoroughly, hoping for even a small clue, but came up empty-handed.

The investigation hit a standstill until May 6th, when conditions were finally ideal to launch a massive search of the river. Water levels had subsided as the heavy runoff from melting snow eased up, and the trees and vegetation in the area hadn't started to bloom yet, making it easier to see. Around 60 people from various agencies assisted in the search, and much of their focus was on the river. Detective Sgt. Matt Denis floated down the river in a raft along with Otto, his dog. Otto was a Korthals Griffon and one of only two cadaver dogs in the state of Vermont. He was also certified by the New England State Police Administrators Conference to find dead bodies. Cadaver dogs are trained to react to chemicals that are released by a dead body – cadaverine and putrescine – and they're trained to do it on land and over water. When a body is underwater, it still releases the same chemicals, and they bubble up to the surface of the water. Once Otto alerted to a spot, it would give the dive team a starting point for their search. While divers waited to see where they would need to dive, around 35 state police recruits conducted a ground search of the area.

About a dozen of Jonathan's friends and family members were watching the search effort when Otto alerted near a tree with a large root ball in the river. The tree was located behind Loomis Trucking, very close to the truck where Jonathan's cell phone had been found. Police brought in an excavator to move the tree so divers would be able to search the area. They were able to lift and roll the tree out of the way, allowing divers to search the root ball and the surrounding area, but they found nothing. Searchers were disappointed; they believed they had been on to something this time. The ground search hadn't produced any evidence, either. For Jonathan's family, disappointment was tempered by the relief that Jonathan hadn't been there. It meant he could still be alive.

Months went by with no movement on the case. January marked an entire year since Jonathan had been seen, and police didn't know much more than they had on the morning he was reported missing. It had been hard on all of his friends and family members, particularly his mother. May Winchell told a reporter that she had started picking up every heads-up penny she found. It was something Jonathan had always done, and whenever May found one, she hoped it would bring her good luck and bring Jonathan home. She believed her son was still alive, and said that two months after he had gone missing, she was certain she heard him shouting her name from the back of a truck she passed on Washington Street. She clung to the hope that she would see him again soon and didn't believe police were on the right track by focusing all of their investigative energy on the river. "I've said that to [investigators] over and over. They say he's in the river, but I don't believe it.

As much as she wanted to believe Jonathan was safe out there somewhere, May admitted that she wondered if the bar fight had something to do with the disappearance. She believed that if her son was no longer alive, it was no accident. He had disappeared shortly after being involved in a bar fight; it seemed to be too much of a coincidence for the two not to be related. In a January 2017 article in the Manchester News, May told the reporter that she had texted her son around 2:00 am and asked how his night was going, and the only reply she got was "Leave me alone." She said she didn't believe it was Jonathan texting her but didn't know who else it could have been. At 2:00 am, Jonathan was still at the bar, and his father was still there as well. No one said anything about Jonathan losing his cell phone; it seems likely that

Jonathan still had his phone that point.

Jonathan's father shared May's belief that their son did not fall into the river and accidentally drown. He didn't share her optimism; he fully believed that Jonathan was dead. "He's not alive. He would have called me or his cousin by now." John's goal was to find out exactly what happened to his son and make sure the perpetrator was held responsible. He was convinced Jonathan was murdered, but he didn't believe that the brawl in the bar had anything to do with it. While he didn't believe most of the rumors that were being spread about the disappearance, he did find one to be credible; he believed Jonathan inadvertently interrupted a drug deal and was killed because of it. He was angry because he was certain there were people in the local area who knew exactly what happened to Jonathan but refused to come forward with that information. He hoped that, by keeping the case in the news, someone reading about the disappearance would realize they might have relevant information for police.

John was not happy with the way police were handling the investigation, and he was not shy in letting it be known. "They're not doing anything, in my opinion." He didn't believe they were making an effort to solve the case and was not at all happy that they spent so much time concentrating on the river.

Police admitted that they still didn't know where Jonathan was, but they disputed the claim that they weren't trying to solve the case. They had invested thousands of hours into the investigation. Detective Sgt. Doug Norton, the lead investigator on the case, told reporters that he could understand why the family was so upset and frustrated, but assured them that he was chasing down every lead that came in.

In March 2016, the family held a fundraiser to try and raise money to hire a private investigator. May noted that the passage of time hadn't made the loss of her son hurt any less, and she was going to do everything she could to find him. "The only thing that keeps me going is hoping and praying that Jonathan is out there alive." She was still unable to sleep most nights, and sometimes the stress was more than she could take. Still, she tried to remain strong, remembering that Jonathan had always told her "It's going to be all right, Mom. It's going to be all right." She just wished she could hear the words directly from him. "I always think about him coming home from work early in the morning, sitting at the table with me, talking to me. I used to talk to him about things I could never talk to anyone about."

Vermont State Police Detective Sgt. Todd Wilkins was assigned to Jonathan's case in April 2016. As he was doing some research and familiarizing himself with the case, he noticed that a quarry close to where Jonathan was last seen had never been searched. While the police had done an extremely thorough investigation of the river in 2014, a quarry off Route 149 wasn't included in the search because it was believed that it had been frozen at the time of Jonathan's disappearance. Detective Sgt. Wilkins did some digging and realized this was not true, the quarry had not been frozen. "Due to the proximity of where he went missing, we needed to put in some time [at the quarry] to make sure he wasn't there." It was located right along Route 149, and easily accessible from the road.

On June 6th, divers from both the Vermont State Police and the New York State Police conducted a search of the unnamed quarry, which was owned by the Sheldon Excavation Company. Nearly a dozen divers spent around five hours in the water but were unable to find anything.

Ruth Varney, who was married to Jonathan's brother, said that this new search had only frustrated her and her husband. "We just feel like they waited so long to do anything, and now all of a sudden they want to do all this stuff. There were a lot of things they didn't hop on when they should, we're just kind of frustrated with the whole system."

In July 2017, Vermont State Police conducted a search of a second quarry, this one located off the York Street Extension in the neighboring town of Poultney. Lt. Reg Trayah told reporters that divers were checking the quarry for anything that might indicate a possible connection to Jonathan's disappearance. He declined to give any more details about what they were looking for but said that they had been given a tip about the place and were following up on it. It was not an easy place to search. Though it only covered a couple of acres, the water was 50 to 60 feet deep and too cloudy for divers to be able to see anything. Loose rocks and other debris in the water made the search quite dangerous and also made it impossible to use sonar equipment. There was simply too much debris for it to be able to discern anything useful.

It's been nearly 10 years since Jonathan walked down Route 149 and disappeared. From the very beginning of the case, police – and Jonathan's friends and family members – had to deal with numerous rumors about what happened that night. Early on, people claimed that Jonathan never made it out of the bar alive that night but had been killed and buried in a new concrete floor in the bar's basement. This one was relatively easy to squash, as no such floor existed.

Rumors that the bar fight was to blame for Jonathan's disappearance were ruled out by police fairly early on. They did extensively interview the man who was involved, but they were confident he had nothing to do with it. When Jonathan's phone was found in a truck at the Loomis Trucking Company parking lot, people began whispering that an employee there was to blame. Detectives interviewed all the employees there and none were ever considered suspects in the case.

Jonathan left the bar with two people, so it was not unexpected when rumors went around claiming that this couple had done something to Jonathan. Police ruled them out fairly early on, though, and Jonathan's family didn't believe they had anything to do with his disappearance. According to John Schaaf, police told him that a series of surveillance cameras show his son walking east that morning, but not making it to a bank where he should have been seen.

A camera that was in front of the Happy Daze pub on Route 149 shows Jonathan, along with two other people, walking east in the direction of Loomis Trucking Company. John said that they were the two people who had offered Jonathan a ride home. But John claimed police told him that the Citizen's Bank surveillance camera, which was across the street from the trucking company, showed only two people. It appeared to be the couple, but there was no sign of Jonathan. This would confirm their story; Jonathan did walk ahead but didn't seem to make it to the truck parking lot. John believes that his son likely tried to walk to a relative's home rather than get a ride with the couple, but ran into some kind of trouble on the way. It's important to note that these details have never been publicly confirmed by police.

If John's information is correct, and Jonathan isn't seen on surveillance camera near the parking lot, how did his phone get into one of the abandoned trucks in the parking lot? It's possible that whoever killed Jonathan worried that police would track his phone to the crime scene, so they planted it in the truck parking lot. It was three days into the search when the phone was found; anyone reading up on the case could have figured out that the truck lot would be the best place to get rid of the phone because police already believed Jonathan had gone there.

When the investigation first started, police believed that Jonathan had most likely fallen into the river and drowned, and they spent months trying to prove this theory. They no longer believe this is the case. Over the past few years, the water levels in the river reached historic lows. If Jonathan had been in the river, they would have found his body by now.

Of all the possible theories, there are only two that police seem to believe are viable at this time: either Jonathan was the victim of foul play, or he voluntarily walked away from his family, friends, and life. No one who knew Jonathan believes that he would have left on his own, and even police seem to think this is a long shot. Foul play is the most likely cause of his disappearance; the question that needs to be answered is who was the person responsible?

Early in the investigation, police stated that they did not think Charles Gould, the man who fought Jonathan that night, had anything to do with his disappearance. He had been seen in his own neighborhood around the time that Jonathan likely went missing, and there is no physical evidence that backs up any claims that he's responsible. He did, however, give conflicting accounts of what happened that night. At one point he claimed it was just a misunderstanding, and the night went on with no hard feelings from either party involved in the fight. Yet he told another reporter that he was kicked out of the bar due to the fight. Still, there is nothing to prove he did anything to Jonathan, and the fight appeared to be a minor one, not one that would cause someone to lie in wait for revenge.

It's possible that Jonathan did run into a random stranger who did something to him. Unfortunately, if that is the case, it's likely that there will never be justice for Jonathan. Police still believe the case can be solved, they are just waiting for someone to come forward with the information they need.

Jonathan Schaff was just 23 years old when he went missing from the New York/Vermont state border in March 2014. He has blue eyes and brown hair, and at the time of his disappearance, he was 6 feet tall and weighed 170 pounds. He wore glasses but they were broken on the night he went missing. When last seen, he was wearing a light blue or gray hooded sweatshirt, a dark brown or black Carhartt jacket, dark blue jeans, and brown work boots. If you have any information about Jonathan, please call the Vermont State Police at 802-773-9101 or the Granville Police Department at 518-642-1414.

Brandon Swanson

Brandon Swanson, a 19-year-old from Marshall, Minnesota, graduated from Marshall High School in June 2007. That fall, he enrolled at the Minnesota West Community and Technical College. He was interested in studying wind turbines, so he chose to attend the Canby campus as it had a Wind Energy Technology course of study. Brandon finished his classes on May 13, 2008, and went out that night with some of his classmates to celebrate the end of the semester.

According to his friends, Brandon had gone to two different parties that night. He had begun his night at a party in Lynd, a small town located about 7 miles to the southwest of his home in Marshall. He later left Lynd and headed 35 miles northwest to Canby, a drive that would have taken around 40 minutes to complete. His classmates would recall that Brandon had a couple of drinks throughout the night, but they were spaced out and he didn't appear to be intoxicated.

Brandon was extremely familiar with the 30-mile drive from Canby to Marshall, as he made it almost every day. The entire drive is done on one road, as the two towns are directly connected by State Highway 68. There is little traffic in the area, and the drive would normally take less than 35 minutes. It's unclear what time Brandon left Canby that night. Some of his friends thought it had been right before midnight, which meant he should have been home around 12:30 am. If his friends are correct about the timeline, there is a substantial chunk of time that is unaccounted for, because Brandon was still on the road more than an hour after he should have arrived in Marshall.

At 1:54 am, Brandon called his parents from his cell phone. He had somehow driven his Chevy Lumina off the road and gotten it stuck in a small ditch. He made repeated attempts at freeing the car but was unable to budge it. He reassured them that he wasn't hurt at all, and there didn't appear to be any damage to the car, either. He just needed help getting it back on the road. He tried to call some of his friends first, but when he couldn't get a hold of anyone who could help him, he called his parents.

Brian and Anita Swanson told their son they would leave right away to help him free the car. Brandon gave them directions to where he was waiting with the car; he was midway between Lynd and Marshall. Going by what he told them, Brian believed that he knew exactly where he needed to go, about a ten-minute drive from their home. In hindsight, this doesn't make much sense, as Brandon should have been approaching Marshall from the northwest. If what he told his parents was correct, he was southwest of Marshall.

It didn't take long for Brian and Anita to arrive at the location they believed Brandon was at, but they were unable to see him or his car. They called Brandon on his cell phone at 2:23 am and told him to keep an eye out for them. After a couple of minutes, they started honking their horn and flashing the headlights of their pickup truck, hoping that Brandon would be able to spot them. They were surprised when Brandon said he couldn't hear their horn or see any lights on the road. They questioned if Brandon had directed them to the correct location, but he was certain that he had.

Changing tactics, they had Brandon start flashing

his headlights. Through the phone, they could hear the clicking noise made as he turned his lights off and on. They peered out into the darkness, hoping to see a glow in the distance, but they still couldn't see a thing. It didn't make sense to them, as they were surrounded by wide, open fields. There was no reason why their view of Brandon's car would be obstructed: if he was on that road, they should have been able to see him.

Brian and Anita had remained on the phone with Brandon the entire time they were searching for him, and he was starting to get aggravated. He was sure he had accurately described his location to his parents, and he couldn't understand why they were unable to follow his directions. They insisted that they were exactly where Brandon told them to go, but Brandon was certain that they were the ones who were confused. Finally, his frustration reached a boiling point, and he hung up on his mother. She called him right back and apologized; given the situation, his frustration was understandable.

Though Brandon had initially thought it would be best for him to stay with his stranded car, he was convinced his parents had somehow ended up in the wrong area and weren't going to be able to find him. No matter how many times he repeated the directions, they didn't seem to understand. Tired of waiting, he decided things would go quicker if he could get to wherever his parents were. He could see lights in the distance coming from what he assumed was Lynd, so he told his parents it would be easier for him to just walk to the town. He had friends who lived in Lynd, so he was familiar with the town. He decided that he would walk to a local bar there, and told his parents to just meet him in the parking lot. He figured there would be no way for him to miss finding them as long as they stayed in one place. It seemed like a foolproof plan. Brian decided that he would drop Annette off at their house, then drive to Lynd and pick up Brandon.

Brandon remained on the phone with his father as he walked, updating him on his progress. He said that he was walking along a gravel road and had taken a shortcut through a field. At one point, he mentioned that he could hear running water coming from somewhere nearby, though he couldn't see anything in the darkness. He just continued to walk towards what he assumed were lights from Lynd.

Brian could do little more than listen as Brandon narrated his journey. Suddenly, around 2:30 am, he heard Brandon cry "Oh, shit!" and the call immediately disconnected. Concerned, he frantically tried to call him back, but he was unable to reach him. He called five or six times in quick succession, but all attempts went straight to Brandon's voicemail without ringing. In order for that to happen, either Brandon had turned his phone off, or something had happened to render the phone inoperable.

At first, Brian was in shock and wasn't sure what to do. He drove back and forth over the same stretch of road numerous times with no success. There was no sign of Brandon or his car. Annette and Brian started calling some of Brandon's friends, and they came out to help look for him. They searched throughout the night, driving down various side roads and scouring the area for any sign of Brandon's car. After a couple of hours went by, they were certain they had thoroughly searched everywhere that Brandon might have gone. They drove back into Lynd and checked the bar parking lot on the off chance that Brandon had somehow managed to make it there, but it was dark and empty. By 6:30 am, Brian and Annette were out of ideas and beginning to panic. They were certain that something had happened to their son. Unsure of what else they could do, they called the Lynd police to report Brandon missing.

Annette and Brian may have been frantic with worry, but it quickly became clear that the police did not share their concern. Brandon was an adult, and he had the right to go missing if he wanted. Anita tried to explain that this wasn't a case of an overprotective parent worrying about a teen who had stayed out too late. Something had happened to Brandon in the instant before his phone went dead, and they were sure it hadn't been anything good. Finally, a couple of hours after they initially reported Brandon missing, police in Lynd agreed to open a missing persons case.

After a perfunctory search around town, police felt confident that Brandon was not in Lynd. A search of the roads leading into the town also failed to yield any evidence. As far as they could tell, Brandon wasn't going to be found anywhere in the vicinity. Brian and Anita continued their search for Brandon's car, certain that they would be able to locate it when the sun came up. But after several hours of searching, they were unable to locate it.

After their unsuccessful search for Brandon, the Lynd police requested the help of Lyon County Sheriff Joel Dahl. He realized immediately that finding Brandon's car would likely be the key to finding Brandon, so the first thing he did was obtain Brandon's cell phone records. He hoped they would help pinpoint exactly where Brandon had been when he spoke with his parents the previous night, and that would give them an idea of where to look next. It was a wise move. When he reviewed the cell records, the sheriff made a startling discovery. Brandon hadn't been found in Lynd because he had never been anywhere near it. The calls he made to his parents the previous night had been made near Taunton, another small town located along State Highway 68. Taunton was on the main route to Canby, but it was northwest of Marshall, and it was 25 miles away from Lynd.

While Taunton was nowhere near Lynd, it made sense that Brandon would have been close to it as he was traveling from home from Canby. Less understandable is why he had still been in that area around 2:00 am. Leaving Canby on Highway 68, it is a 13-mile drive to Taunton, and it would normally take about 15 minutes. From Taunton, Brandon only had another 17 miles to go before he would be in Marshall. If Brandon left Canby around midnight as his friends believed, it somehow took him nearly 2 hours to drive only 13 miles.

Armed with the information gleaned from the cell phone records, the search for Brandon was shifted to the area surrounding Taunton. It didn't take long for investigators to locate the car. It had been abandoned in a ditch off a gravel road, just over the Lincoln County line and about a mile to the north of Highway 68. The car was located in Lincoln County, within the boundaries of the small town of Porter. Since the car was found in his jurisdiction, Lincoln County Sheriff Jack Vizecky joined the investigation at that point. He noted that the car was off the side of a field approach, and had gotten hung up on a sharp incline. While there didn't appear to be any damage to the car, only two of its tires were touching the ground. Brandon would not have been able to get the traction he needed to get the car out of the ditch.

Investigators searched the inside of the car thoroughly, and they found nothing that suggested Brandon had been injured. It was clear Brandon had accurately described exactly what had happened when he called his parents; the only thing he was wrong about was his location. He told his parents he could see lights in the distance that he thought were coming from Lynd, but it was obvious now that he had not been anywhere near there. Investigators needed to figure out what Brandon had actually been looking at so they could determine the direction he had been walking when his parents lost contact with him.

The car's resting place had been surrounded by grass and gravel, and there were no discernible tracks to show which direction Brandon had walked when he left the car. Further analysis of his cell phone records showed that his call to his parents had been routed through a cell phone tower near Minneota, another small town on Highway 68 located about 4 miles southeast of Taunton. According to his cell phone provider, Brandon had been within 5 miles of that tower when he was on the phone, allowing them to narrow down the search area. Part of this search area extended into Yellow Medicine County, bringing a third jurisdiction into the investigation.

Investigators noticed that a red light on the top of a grain elevator in Taunton could be seen from where Brandon's car was found. It was possible Brandon had seen this light and assumed it was coming from Lynd. If this was the light that he was heading for, he would have been walking northwest when he left his car. The fact that he was on foot meant that the distance he could have covered was limited. His parents spent a total of 47 minutes on the phone with him, and he had been sitting inside his car for part of that time.

An extensive ground search was launched, with searchers concentrating on the area that had been pinpointed by Brandon's cell phone records. Helicopters flew over the area, looking for anything that might be relevant. A team of bloodhounds was brought in, and they were quick to pick up on Brandon's scent. They followed a scent trail for nearly three miles as it skirted past fields and headed in a west-northwest direction to an abandoned farm. The dogs continued past the farm and headed along the Yellow Medicine River. When they reached a certain point, their actions seemed to indicate that Brandon had entered the river at that spot. The water ranged from knee-high to around 15 feet; even if Brandon had entered the water it wouldn't necessarily mean he drowned. It was possible that he could have made it across to the other side, but dogs were unable to follow the trail any further.

Worried that Brandon may have fallen into the water and drowned, the area along the two-mile stretch of river was searched extensively. If Brandon had drowned, his body would have been washed downstream, but searchers found nothing at all. Sheriff Jack walked up and down the riverbank for 30 days with no results. Investigators determined it was unlikely Brandon had drowned there, as his body should have been located if that were the case.

The official search for Brandon was suspended after a week, but his family continued to search on their own. On May 24th and again on June 7th, around 100 volunteers joined Brandon's parents in searching areas to the south and east of Porter. Some of the searchers used ATVs to be able to cover more distance, while others walked or rode horses. Despite their extensive effort, they found no sign of Brandon. At the end of June, Texas EquuSearch offered their assistance, and the family gratefully accepted. They searched the river using sonar equipment, then used remote-controlled drones to conduct an aerial search. Unfortunately, their search also failed to find anything. Determined to find their son, his parents held a hog roast on July 13th to raise money for their search fund. A local financial institution announced they would match any funds that were raised, and the search effort continued.

The search effort resumed in the fall once all the fields in the area had been harvested. Cadaver dogs were brought in to assist, and though they seemed to be following a scent trail into the area to the northwest of Porter, they eventually lost the scent, and nothing was found. When winter came, bringing along snowstorms and frigid temperatures, the search was suspended once again. By this time, 122 square miles had been searched without turning up any trace of Brandon. A tip line that had been set up brought in 90 leads, but none of them led to Brandon. All told, the search had involved 500 volunteers, 34 dog handlers from nine different states, and countless hours of hard work.

Six months after Brandon disappeared, investigators didn't seem to be any closer to finding him. Sheriff Jack Vizecky admitted that they had no idea if Brandon was alive or dead; it was a frustrating case. He didn't believe Brandon had drowned, as he was confident that his body would have been found if that was the case. He noted that they couldn't rule out foul play, but there was nothing to indicate it had occurred. Unless they found evidence to the contrary, Brandon's case would remain categorized as a missing person investigation, not a homicide.

Brandon's case was handed over to the Minnesota Bureau of Criminal Investigation in 2010; from that point on, they would be the lead agency on the case. They focused their investigation on the area around Mud Creek, a tributary of the Yellow Medicine River located directly north of Taunton and to the northeast of Porter. While they didn't find anything, they continued to search there periodically over the next few years.

While there are a lot of unknowns about Brandon's disappearance, there are two that are particularly perplexing: What happened to Brandon in the seconds after his "Oh, shit!" exclamation? And where was he when it happened? If police could discover the answers to these questions, they would almost certainly be able to find Brandon. Despite all the searches that have been conducted over the years, the only real piece of evidence found was Brandon's car. His cell phone, wallet, glasses, car keys, and clothing have never turned up.

Many theories have been put forth to explain Brandon's sudden disappearance. Some people believe he may have staged his own disappearance, but it seems highly unlikely. Brandon was a good student, and he had just completed a wind energy certificate course. He had no problems at home or school, and had been looking forward to transferring to a school in Iowa a few months later to continue his studies. He wasn't in any kind of legal trouble and he was close with his family. The circumstances surrounding his disappearance also point away from it being a staged event. Purposely getting your car stuck on the side of the road, calling your parents for help, then staying on the phone with them for nearly an hour until pretending to experience some kind of unsettling event is simply not plausible.

Another theory is that Brandon was struck and killed by a car while walking, and the driver panicked and hid his body. While there have been a handful of cases where this has happened, it is doubtful that Brandon met that fate. He told his father he had been cutting through fields, not walking along the road. This is supported by both cell phone records and the path taken by tracking dogs, both of which indicate Brandon was not on the road. Additionally, if this had happened, there would have been evidence left at the accident scene. Blood, tire marks, and possibly pieces of the vehicle should have been found, but extensive searching produced no evidence of this.

Foul play is possible, but unlikely. The area Brandon was in was sparsely populated: Taunton, for example, had a population of 135 at the time, and only 175 people lived in Porter. Much of the area is farmland, and houses are few and far between. It would have been almost impossible for someone to lie in wait for Brandon; there was no way anyone in the Porter area could have known ahead of time that he was going to get his car stuck in a ditch and proceed on foot. Likewise, it's probably safe to rule out the theory that this was a crime of opportunity. The chance that someone just happened to see Brandon walking in the dark and decided to kill him is slim, especially when considering the small population size.

It's possible – and quite probable – that Brandon's disappearance was nothing more than a tragic accident. He was attempting to make his way, on foot, through darkened fields and side roads. There were no streetlights to guide him, and no houses or businesses he could use as landmarks. He was surrounded by corn and soybean fields, and they would have all looked alike in the dark. He had mentioned to his father that he could hear running water while he was walking, though he didn't seem concerned about it. It's possible that he did slip into the river at some point, but it wouldn't necessarily mean that he drowned. He could have gotten up out of the water, disoriented but still very much alive. He may have been able to keep walking for a while, but he would have been wet and cold, and likely would have succumbed to hypothermia eventually. While the temperature had been relatively mild during daylight hours, it dropped below 40 degrees in the overnight hours. The temperature doesn't have to sink below freezing to be deadly. Most cases of hypothermia occur between 30 and 50 degrees. It's quite possible that Brandon did die of exposure, but the fact remains that his body has never been found. While some hypothermia victims have been known to burrow or hide in small spaces immediately before death, cadaver dogs should have been able to locate him if they were searching in the correct area.

Some people have suggested the possibility that Brandon, unable to continue walking, laid down in a field and died, and his body was later run over by a piece of farm equipment. They point out that police were never able to access all the fields in the area when they were searching, and believe that a landowner could be trying to keep the death hidden. In a case with so many unknowns, it's a possible scenario, but it doesn't seem very likely. Although this was a sparsely populated area, Brandon's disappearance was well-publicized, and the search effort was extensive. From the beginning, investigators believed Brandon had likely died an accidental death somewhere in the area. If a farmer discovered Brandon's body in a field, it wouldn't have immediately elevated him to a murder suspect and there would be little reason for him to hide the body.

There are wild animals in Minnesota, including dangerous ones like black bears and large wildcats, but an attack by one of those would have left some kind of evidence behind. If Brandon had run into a wild animal, it could have been enough for him to cry out in fear, but it wouldn't have immediately disabled his phone. If there had been an animal attack, Brandon's keys, phone, and glasses should have been found, as well as shreds of clothing and blood evidence.

Brandon's ultimate fate isn't the only question that

remains in this investigation, but unless Brandon can be found alive, we may never know the answer: How could Brandon have been so wrong about where he was when he got his car stuck? He made the drive from Marshall to Canby and back again every day when he went to class, it seems impossible that he could have been so confused. Something had to be going on that night to make that drive different from all the other times he had done it. Brandon had consumed alcohol that night, and though his friends didn't believe he was intoxicated, it's possible he drank just enough to make himself paranoid. If he was worried that he might get pulled over, he may have decided that staying off the highway was his safest course of action. Normally, he would have taken Highway 68 from Canby all the way home to Marshall. It was a quick and direct route, but not necessarily the only route. Although it would take much longer, it was possible to use gravel field access roads to skirt around the highway. Brandon abandoned his car on one of these gravel roads, and he had been walking on a gravel road at one point when he was on the phone with his father, so we know for a fact that Brandon wasn't on the highway at that point. While the drive from Canby to Marshall could be completed without making any turns if the highway was used, trying to navigate between the two towns using field access roads would have required making numerous 90-degree turns; if plotted on a map, this route would resemble a staircase. Brandon would have headed east for a block, then south for a block, then east again. This pattern would repeat the entire way home. It would explain why his car was found on one of these field access roads; he got hung up in a small ditch while attempting to turn. It would also explain why Brandon told his parents he was between Lynd and Marshall. If he had properly navigated the gravel roads in a staircase shape, he would have ended up south of Marshall, near Highway 23 in Lynd. He may have simply underestimated the amount of time it would take to drive that distance. All the field access roads look similar, especially in the dark. Brandon may have assumed he had traveled much further than he actually had.

If Brandon had decided to avoid the highway completely, it would also explain the large time discrepancy between when his friends said he left that party and when he called his parents for help. His friends said he left the party around midnight. Using the highway, he would have been home around 12:45 am. He started making phone calls to some of his friends around 1:15 am, which is believed to be the time that he got his car stuck after failing to properly navigate a turn on a dark field access road. He had been driving for at least an hour and probably did believe that he was close to Lynd at that point. The fact that he was nowhere near there could be because he was driving extremely slow on gravel roads, or it could have been because he had been going in circles and hadn't realized it. With no landmarks, and with all the fields he passed looking the same, Brandon simply had no idea where he was.

Brandon Victor Swanson was just 19 years old when he went missing from Taunton, Minnesota in May 2008. He has blue eyes and brown hair, and at the time of his disappearance, he was 5 feet 6 inches tall and weighed 125 pounds. He was last seen wearing a pair of blue jeans, a blue striped polo shirt, a black hooded sweatshirt that zipped up the front, and a white Minnesota Twins baseball cap. He was also wearing eyeglasses with silver frames and a sterling silver chain. He was carrying a black Motorola cell phone, his wallet, and car keys. If you have any information on Brandon, please call the Minnesota Bureau of Criminal Apprehension at 877-996-6222 or email them at bca.coldcase@state.mn.us.

Tabitha Tuders

April 29, 2004, started as a normal day in the Tuders family's home in Nashville, Tennessee. Debra Tuders woke up first, getting ready for work in the predawn darkness. When she got out of bed, she had to step over her 13-year-old daughter, Tabitha, who was curled up on the floor at the foot of her parents' bed. Tabitha had her own room and a purple canopy bed she loved, but she rarely spent a full night in it. She went to sleep each night in her bed, but more often than not she would wake up in the middle of the night, drag her blanket into her parents' room, and curl up on a makeshift bed of pillows on their floor. It just made her feel secure. It may have been odd, but she wasn't hurting anything, so her parents let her do it. Debra was used to stepping over her as she got ready for work, it was just another part of the morning routine.

Debra worked as a cook in the cafeteria of a local elementary school, and always left home around 6:00 am to get there on time. Her husband, Bo, was a short-haul trucker for a local lumber company and didn't leave the house until 7:00 am. Each morning, the last thing he did before leaving the house was wake Tabitha up so she could get ready for school. He told her he loved her and would see her that evening. When he left, she was still in her nightgown and somewhat groggy, but she assured him she was awake. She needed to catch the bus to Bailey Middle School at 8:00 am, and the bus stop was a five-minute walk from her home. She would leave each morning at 7:50 am. Her mother didn't want her to leave any earlier because she didn't want her to spend any time alone at the bus stop. Leaving at 7:50 am usually meant that there were others already at the stop when Tabitha got there.

Normally, Tabitha would have been alone in the house from the time her father left for work until she left to walk to the bus stop. Things were a little different that morning, though. Her 21-year-old sister, Jamie, had spent the previous night at her parents' home, along with her two young children. They were all still sleeping when Tabitha got up, and they didn't wake up until after she had already left for school.

Tabitha got dressed in a pair of Mudd jeans and a light blue shirt, and then pulled on a pair of white Reebok sneakers. She left her home on Lilliam Street at 7:50 am like she always did, heading for her bus stop a short walk away at the corner of South 14th Street and Boscobel Street. She was carrying a sheet of paper with her, most likely the report card she had proudly brought home for her parents to sign the day before. She had gotten straight As. When she got close to the first bus stop, just a block from her house, there was no one there so she headed for the second bus stop another block away. This was a standard safety precaution her mother had taught her so she would never be lingering on a corner by herself.

When Debra got home from work around 1:00 pm, the house was empty. This was normal; Tabitha would usually come home at 4:00 pm. When 4:00 pm came and went without Tabitha skipping through the front door, Debra started to get worried but figured the bus was just running a few minutes late.

As the minutes continued to tick by with no sign of her daughter, Debra decided to make the three-block walk down to the bus stop. She checked with a neighbor, but she hadn't seen the teen either. She accompanied Debra down to the bus stop. It was possible the bus just hadn't dropped her off yet, or maybe she had stopped to chat with a friend and lost track of time. There was no one at the bus stop when Debra got there, and her concern for her daughter was escalating. Tabitha had never before been late coming home from school. Unsure what to do next, Debra drove over to the middle school. Although she knew it was unlikely, perhaps Tabitha had some sort of afterschool activity and had simply forgotten to let her know ahead of time. That hope was quickly dashed, as Debra found the doors to the school had already been shut and locked.

Bo got home from work at 5:00 pm to find that his daughter hadn't come home from school and his wife was in a state of panic. It was a situation no parent is prepared to deal with. He and Debra drove back to Bailey Middle School and pounded on the locked doors. They were able to get the attention of a janitor, who unlocked the door and allowed them into the school. They frantically raced through the empty hallways of the school but found no sign of Tabitha. They did find a teacher, however, and explained to him what was going on. The news he had for them wasn't good: Tabitha hadn't been at school at all that day. Fighting hysteria, Bo and Debra knew that could only mean one thing. Their daughter had been abducted.

Tabitha was the youngest of three children. Her older brother was 24 years old and her sister was 21. Though she was much younger than her two siblings, she had been a planned baby. Her parents had talked about having a third child, but the timing never seemed right. When Debra started getting older, she decided it was time. She didn't want to wake up one day and realize she was too old to have another child. When she and Bo learned that they were expecting a girl, they decided to name her Brittany. This lasted until the day Tabitha was born. She simply didn't look like a Brittany; she was most definitely a Tabitha. A minister later told them that the name meant "gazelle," certainly fitting for Tabitha and her limitless energy.

Tabitha had been a chubby baby, close to 10 pounds when she was born. Despite this, she grew into a petite teenager, standing near 5'0" and weighing only 90 pounds. When her sister was still living at home, Tabitha shared a room with her, but she wasn't always happy about it. The sisters weren't particularly close, likely due to the large gap in their ages, and Tabitha didn't like how messy her sister kept the room. Tabitha wanted things to be immaculate. Not long before she went missing, her father had renovated her bedroom for her, everything from new walls to a new floor. She had been allowed to pick out her new bedroom furniture and had selected a canopy bed with a lilac canopy that she loved.

It was clear from looking around Tabitha's bedroom that she was not a young teenager trying to act older than her years. She still bought most of her clothes from the children's department. Her room was filled with teddy bears and other stuffed animals, and she had a collection of G-rated movies. She didn't have a large makeup collection and rarely wore any except for peach-flavored lip gloss. She wore her hair straight and long, and it was constantly falling in front of her face. She would automatically reach up and push it back as if on autopilot.

Tabitha was in seventh grade at Bailey Middle School, where she was well-liked and was an excellent student. She and her best friend would sometimes volunteer to help out in the school library, fighting over who would get to use the electric stapler. The librarian recalled that Tabitha usually won. She never got into any trouble at school, and she seemed to be a happy and well-adjusted teenager, with nothing to indicate any problems at home or with friends.

About six months before she went missing, Tabitha had started attending church with her best friend's family. It was something she decided to do on her own, and she seemed to enjoy it. She loved to sing and joined the church choir, and volunteered at a spaghetti dinner the church held. The Sunday before she went missing, she had received a $20 prize at Sunday School for memorizing the Ten Commandments. Investigators would find the money in her room, untouched.

Tabitha had a soft spot for elderly people and had befriended an 82-year-old woman who lived nearby. She called her Grandma and would visit her a couple of times a week to read to her. She seemed to enjoy going out of her way to make other people happy. One day, about two months before she went missing, she had taken her lunch money and gone to the Dollar General store where she bought a garden stone decorated with frogs. She didn't buy it for herself, but for the mother of one of her friends. She knew the woman collected frogs and thought she would like it. She was known for having a big heart and always wanted to help others. When a neighbor's air conditioner broke on a sweltering summer day, Tabitha had immediately invited the woman – and her dogs – to come to her house to cool off.

She was also extremely close with her parents, preferring to spend her free time with them. She would go to Saturday night car races with them all the time, cheering on her older brother who was one of the drivers. Often, some of her friends would go with her, but Tabitha went even if they didn't. She was exceptionally close with her mother, and the two were almost always together. She rarely went anywhere without her mom, but if she did, her mother knew where she was going and when she would be back. If she had been an unreliable child, the fact that she hadn't returned home from school on time may not have been quite so terrifying to her parents. But this was a child who had never spent any extended amount of time away from home, had never been on a plane, and had never expressed any inclination to run. As they left the school that afternoon without their daughter, Bo and Debra were almost paralyzed with fear.

The couple raced home and called the police to report their daughter missing. When an officer responded 45 minutes later, they told him that Tabitha had never done anything like this, and they were absolutely positive that she would not run away from home. Someone must have taken her. The officer wasn't so sure. Tabitha was a 13-year-old girl, and they can often act in unpredictable ways. Even the most obedient child can turn wild once the teenage years hit. Since no one had witnessed an abduction, the case didn't meet the criteria necessary for law enforcement to issue an Amber Alert. But there was no evidence that Tabitha was a runaway, either. With nothing to go on one way or another, police launched a search in the neighborhood. They also alerted the National Center for Missing and Exploited Children about Tabitha, and called the local news media so they could help get the word out on the evening news that night.

Marlene Pardue, a close family friend, was a lieutenant with Metro police at the time, and Debra called her to let her know what was going on. Marlene and her husband, also a police officer, went to the house to see if they could offer their friends any help. As a friend of the family, she knew Tabitha wasn't the kind of girl to run away. Yet she also understood the way law enforcement approached the case and told a local reporter that missing teenagers tend to get treated differently. "The challenge was her age. Age 12 and under is regarded as a probable abduction or lost child." Once they hit the teen years, the tendency is to treat the child as a runaway, because in the overwhelming majority of cases, they are runaways.

Whether they thought Tabitha ran away or not, within the first few hours of the search, more than a hundred officers were involved – nearly a third of the Nashville officers who were on duty at the time responded to the call. Officers conducted a door-to-door search in the neighborhood and searched all empty buildings and businesses in a two-mile radius. They tried to get a helicopter to assist from the air, but the weather got progressively worse as the night went on and their helicopters were grounded. Hours passed, and they hadn't found any sign of Tabitha. More than a dozen officers kept searching overnight, hoping to find anything that could point them in the right direction.

Friends and relatives also joined in the search for Tabitha, and their numbers grew as word got out. Debra was touched by the fact that so many people she didn't know had come out to look for her daughter. Knowing there was no way to adequately thank them for their time, she and Bo kept a steady stream of coffee brewing for them. Yet even as the community came together to offer their support, there were whispered concerns about the general safety of the area. East Nashville has undergone a gentrification process over the past decade, but in 2003 it was still a somewhat gritty environment. Just a year and a half earlier, a 16-year-old girl living two blocks away from the Tuders had been murdered. The cases were not related, and the murderer had been caught and pleaded guilty. Still, seeing a tragedy befall another young girl on the same street was tough, especially for parents. They began wondering if it might be safer to move somewhere else.

One of the biggest problems police faced was the time difference between when Tabitha was last seen and when she was reported missing. Since her parents had assumed that she had made it safely to school that morning, it wasn't until late afternoon that they realized something was wrong. By the time police were called in, Tabitha hadn't been seen for over 10 hours. If she had been abducted, she could have been anywhere in the state by then – or in one of 13 other states. It put the investigators at a huge disadvantage. Time is the most critical factor in child abduction cases: almost 75% of children who are abducted and then murdered are killed within three hours of going missing. It is a sobering statistic.

By Wednesday morning, they were no closer to finding Tabitha, and she had been missing for more than 24 hours. Detectives continued canvassing the neighborhood, interviewing anyone who knew her. When they spoke with school administrators, they were surprised to learn that Tabitha, though a good student, did not have a very good attendance record. So far that year, she had been absent 18 times, and only six had been excused absences. Her absenteeism the year before was even greater. LuAnn Landrum, the principal at Bailey Middle School, said that she spoke with Tabitha's parents and they were aware of her absences, but they hadn't sent in notes for all of them, which is why some were considered unexcused. While the number of times she missed school may have raised some eyebrows among the investigators, they focused on the fact that she had never failed to come home in the afternoon before.

Five detectives were assigned to work on the case full-time. These detectives believed there were people in the community who had useful information but were not coming forward with it. Noting that Tabitha had disappeared on a sunny morning, at a time when kids were waiting at bus stops and parents were driving to work, they urged anyone who may have seen anything even slightly out of the ordinary to call. It seemed impossible that the teen could have been abducted at that time of day without someone noticing.

As they continued to interview people, a boy came forward to say he had seen something concerning. The 11-year-old was also a student at Bailey Middle School, and he had been waiting at the bus stop that Tabitha was walking towards. He told detectives that he saw her walking down the hill toward the stop on Boscobel Street. When she was about 30 yards from the bus stop, a red car pulled over next to her and she got inside. The car had come from 14th Street and was headed towards 15th Street when it pulled over. After Tabitha got in, the driver, a dark-skinned male wearing a backward baseball cap, had then turned the car around and headed back up the hill. If true, this was a tip that could potentially solve the case. Yet police said they did not find the boy to be credible, and they hadn't been able to confirm anything he said. Still, if he was correct, he was the last person to see Tabitha before she vanished, and his potential sighting would be reinvestigated numerous times over the years.

Whether Tabitha got into a red car continued to be hotly debated, but tracking dogs seemed to indicate that a car – red or otherwise – may have been involved. Detectives brought in a couple of tracking dogs to assist in the search, and they were given a stuffed animal of Tabitha's so they could search for her scent. The dogs took off, turned onto Boscobel Street from 14th Street, and headed down Boscobel in the direction of the 15th Street bus stop. They then abruptly stopped three or four houses away from the bus stop, turned around, and went back the way they came. This was consistent with the boy's account of seeing Tabitha get into a car. Her parents were adamant that she would never have gotten into a car with anyone she didn't know unless she had explicit permission from her parents. She once refused an offer of a ride from one of her mother's friends, telling the woman her mom hadn't told her in advance that it would be okay to accept the ride.

There were a couple of witnesses who had seen Tabitha as she made her way toward the bus stop, and police believed these were credible sightings. It appeared that Tabitha had left her home at her usual time and was making her way to her bus stop, but something happened before she could get there. No one could say if she had been taken by force or had willingly gone somewhere with someone.

Although they still said they had no signs of foul play, detectives noted that each day Tabitha remained missing raised their concern for her. Though she was a teenager, she was a young teenager. She couldn't drive and had no access to a car. If she was no longer in the area, someone else would have had to assist her. There had only been a few possible sightings reported; investigators had followed up on each one but determined that none of them were Tabitha.

A search of Tabitha's bedroom produced a small handwritten note reading "T.D.T. -N- M.T.L." in Tabitha's handwriting. Detectives assumed that "M.T.L" was a romantic interest of Tabitha's, but her parents were unaware of anyone with those initials, and their daughter definitely didn't have a boyfriend. Bo recalled a couple of occasions when a boy had called the house to speak with Tabitha, but she had told her father to say she wasn't home. She simply hadn't reached a boy-crazy stage yet, though her parents couldn't rule out the possibility that she may have had a schoolgirl crush on one of her classmates and just hadn't told them.

Tabitha didn't own a cell phone, and police went through the phone records for her home telephone looking for anything out of the ordinary, but found nothing to indicate that Tabitha had been calling anyone, male or female, that her parents weren't aware of. Later, detectives would say that they believed the initials referred to the 18-year-old son of a family friend. He had been in school the day she went missing, and didn't have a car at the time. Police determined that he was not involved in her disappearance, and likely was unaware that the younger girl even had a crush on him.

A week after Tabitha went missing, some out-of-state volunteers arrived in Nashville to assist in the search. They were led by Craig Akers, who had founded the Shawn Hornbeck Foundation after his son went missing seven months earlier in Missouri. He, along with five Foundation members and three search dogs, searched the wooded areas near each of the two bus stops on Boscobel Street. They were joined by members of the Laura Recovery Center from Texas, which had been established by the parents of Laura Smither after she was abducted and murdered in 1997. They handed out flyers to motorists who drove by the bus stops each morning, hoping that one of them may have seen something pertinent to the investigation. Bo and Debra were very grateful for the help, noting that Craig had taken time out of his ongoing search for his own son to help them. He was pleased he could offer some assistance. Although they didn't turn up any new evidence, the search did help keep Tabitha's name in the media.

Two weeks after she went missing, police got a tip that Tabitha and a friend had used an East Nashville Public Library computer to access an internet chat room, making some wonder if she had been planning to meet up with someone she met online. They removed the computer terminal in question, and computer experts examined the contents of the hard drive in an attempt to find information relevant to the case. Unfortunately, they didn't find any useful information, and the computer was returned to the library. She did not have access to a home computer, so detectives felt confident that the internet had not played any part in her disappearance. Though they said they couldn't completely rule out anything at this point, there was nothing to suggest someone she met online abducted her.

Bo and Debra were surprised to learn that there were at least five registered sex offenders living within a mile of their home. The closest one lived less than 740 feet away. Police were in the process of making contact with each one and questioning them, but weeks into the investigation admitted that they had not been able to clear all of them yet. For Tabitha's parents, it was an uncomfortable revelation. The short, three-block walk to the bus stop wasn't quite as safe as they assumed.

In the middle of May, Bo and Debra traveled to New York City to tape a segment for "The John Walsh Show." Even though they were only gone for a couple of days, Debra dreaded being away from home. She was terrified that she was going to miss a call from Tabitha and had certainly never envisioned that she would one day be appearing on national television. Still, she knew that the publicity could help bring Tabitha home, and she was gratified when John Walsh said he was certain Tabitha wasn't a runaway. Three weeks into the disappearance, Metro police still believed there was a chance that Tabitha was voluntarily missing.

Tabitha's friends and family continued to insist that the teen had not run away from home. She had no reason to. She had gotten straight As on her last report card and had been looking forward to an upcoming class trip to Kentucky Kingdom. The trip went on, as planned, on May 17th. Many of Tabitha's classmates wore buttons with her picture on them to honor her when they went.

Bo had to go back to work three weeks after Tabitha disappeared. He couldn't afford to take any more time off and was torn between earning a living and finding his daughter. Debra did not return to work and would continue to focus all her time and energy on looking for Tabitha.

At the end of May, Charles Jones, the founder of Project Safe Child, arrived in Nashville to offer his assistance in the search. Recognizing that most police departments have very little experience in long-term missing children cases, Jones created a service to fill the void. He never charged a fee, paying for the organization out of his own pocket. He would coordinate the efforts of families, volunteers, law enforcement, and nationwide missing person organizations to increase their efficiency. He had become somewhat of a legend in the field, and his help was greatly appreciated. He helped the volunteers at the search command post to organize things more efficiently and develop a better system for logging tips that were called in.

From the very beginning of the investigation, law enforcement had been aware of the fact that Tabitha's older brother Kevin didn't have a pristine criminal background, but this wasn't picked up on by the media until a couple of months after Tabitha went missing. Kevin Tuders had been arrested two years earlier, at the age of 22, as part of a 2001 sting operation on a Nashville prostitution ring. He had been one of a large number of men who were arrested while chauffeuring prostitutes to their customers. 34 people were indicted in what was deemed to be the largest-ever investigation into Nashville's escort industry. In February 2002, Kevin pleaded guilty to charges of money laundering and promoting prostitution, and he was sentenced to three years of unsupervised probation.

Police spokesman Don Aaron told the media that Metro police had been aware of Kevin's past and had questioned him early on in their investigation, right after Tabitha went missing. Based on these interviews with him, they did not believe that Kevin was involved in his sister's disappearance. Aaron also said that there was nothing indicating anyone connected to the escort industry had been involved in the disappearance either. The Tuders family decline to publicly comment on Kevin's past crime, but a family friend told reporters that Kevin had been very remorseful about his crime and had cleaned up his act. He did not have any further run-ins with the law.

It wouldn't be the last time a close family member would go through a trial-by-media in Tabitha's disappearance. Her sister, Jamie, found herself under close scrutiny after police said she failed three of the four lie detector/voice stress tests she was given. She said the only reason she failed was because she had been extremely nervous after investigators told her that her children would be taken away from her if she didn't pass. Police would dispute this, claiming that there had never been any threat of her losing her children. Either way, there were some who wondered if she had been somehow involved. Her boyfriend at the time did match the description of the driver of the red car Tabitha's classmate claimed he saw her get into, though he had an alibi for the morning of the disappearance, and didn't have a car. There were whispers that he had access to a red car, and he certainly knew what time Tabitha left for the bus each morning. Her parents had insisted from the start that she never would have gotten into a car with a stranger, leaving open the possibility that she may have been picked up by someone she knew.

In July, Metro police added investigators to the case and started using some of their patrol officers to help seek out leads. Deborah Faulkner, the acting police chief, told the media that she was concerned because there wasn't much information coming in about the case. She had been under fire since the beginning of the investigation by people who didn't believe the police department had taken the investigation seriously, and now it looked like the case was going cold.

The news media had been extremely critical of the police department, particularly the fact that an Amber Alert had never been issued when Tabitha went missing. Detectives pointed out that the case hadn't met the criteria necessary to issue such an alert, and they were correct. The media also publicly condemned acting police chief Deborah Faulkner, as she had never taken the time to sit down and discuss the case with Bo and Debra, and at one point was unable to name the detective that was in charge of the investigation. As far as the media was concerned, the renewed interest in the case had come only when Faulkner realized she was unlikely to be offered a permanent position as police chief due to the way Tabitha's high-profile case had been handled. It's important to note, however, that Bo and Debra were always quick to praise law enforcement and felt like they were doing everything they could to find Tabitha. While there were times when they felt frustrated, especially when police seemed to think their daughter was a runaway, if they had any harsh criticism, they kept it to themselves. Their public support of law enforcement never wavered.

Detectives renewed their effort to identify and track down all registered sex offenders in the area. Beat officers, who did not normally do any independent investigations, started questioning people in the hopes that they could identify potential sightings of the missing girl. People who lived in Tabitha's neighborhood were re-interviewed, with investigators concentrating on those who believed they had seen the young girl as she walked towards the bus stop that morning.

Anthony Manning was one of the residents who claimed to have seen Tabitha. He lived on Boscobel Street and had been looking out his front door the Tuesday morning she went missing. He recalled seeing a blonde girl acting in a way he felt was suspicious. He later identified the girl as Tabitha and told investigators that he saw her heading for the top of the hill when she stopped and appeared to be looking at something on the corner of South 14th and Boscobel Streets. She started to cross the street, then changed her mind and walked back down the street. She was walking slowly and had a paper in her hand that she was looking at. Since there had been some recent break-ins in the neighborhood, he was concerned that she was up to no good. He told a reporter he had wondered what she was doing. "She was looking kind of suspicious." He changed his mind as she got closer, though. "I thought she had probably missed the school bus because there wasn't anyone else out but her."

From his description, it appeared Tabitha had initially walked towards the first bus stop on Boscobel Street, but hesitated when she didn't see any other children there. Like her mother had told her to do if no one was there, she then headed for the second bus stop. This would have taken her directly past Manning's home. He was unable to tell investigators if she made it to the bus stop or not. Once he realized she had probably missed her bus and wasn't looking to break into any homes, he lost interest and shut his front door. Sadly, if he had continued to watch for another minute or so, he may have been able to confirm or discredit the information about Tabitha getting into a red car. According to the boy who reported the sighting, it had taken place not too long after Tabitha would have walked past Manning's house.

Oh July 15th, police announced that they were shifting their focus from a possible runaway case to one of possible foul play. They noted that, while they still did not have any evidence to prove Tabitha had been hurt or abducted, the fact that she had been missing this long with no contact and no confirmed sightings led them to believe that she hadn't left voluntarily. It was what her friends and family had been saying all along. When Tabitha left for school that morning, she didn't have anything with her except what she would normally take to school. She didn't pack a bag with any extra clothes, and all of her belongings were still in her room, including money. If she had planned on running away, she would have at least taken her money.

Once they announced foul play seemed likely,

detectives went back to the very beginning of the investigation and basically started over from scratch. They conducted a massive ground search for Tabitha, aided by dogs who had been trained to track the scent of decomposition and find dead bodies. They swarmed over the entire neighborhood, and some residents were surprised to wake up to the sight of officers and dogs roaming through their front yards. Debra was grateful for the renewed effort to find her daughter, but it was' bittersweet. "I think that if they'd done this sooner, maybe we'd have her back by now."

It was a massive search. Arthur Wolff, a retired police officer from Fort Lauderdale and an instructor for the National Association of Search and Rescue, joined the search along with Jason, his 12-year-old German shepherd. Jason, a cadaver dog, had been trained by using the command "find prunes." Wolff said this was so no one else could inadvertently give him orders. Another dog handler had trained his dog to respond to Arabic commands. "If you have multiple dogs working a scene, it makes sense to give them individual commands." It was a wise tactic. Neighbors, especially children, were extremely interested in the dogs, and many couldn't help but cry out to them in excitement. The dogs had an amazing ability to block out the cacophony of sounds, responding only to their handlers as they went about the three-day search. Unfortunately, they didn't find anything relevant to the investigation.

The ground search turned up a few articles of clothing and a pocketknife, but it was later determined that none of the items collected were related to Tabitha's case. Helicopters flew over the Cumberland River, looking for anything out of place. The aerial search was supplemented by three Office of Emergency Management personnel who used a boat to search the river. A cadaver dog named Sydney joined them in the boat, but she didn't have any more luck than the dogs who had been searching on land.

Monday, July 28th was graduation day for the 35 new recruits of the Metro Police Department. For each of the 35 newly minted officers, their first assignment would be to help in another large-scale search for Tabitha. The search covered a wooded area of an East Nashville park, and police methodically searched through a four-mile stretch of the Shelby River bottoms. No new evidence was found.

In August, students at Bailey Middle School were sent home with notes for their parents concerning the investigation into Tabitha's disappearance. The notes were a plea for help in finding the teen and included a photocopy and description of a potential piece of evidence that had been found during a search of Tabitha's bedroom. One of the items was what appeared to be a business card. It had a picture of Winnie the Pooh hugging a large pink heart and included Tabitha's name, address, and phone number. The phrase "sexy girl" had been printed on the card, but had been crossed out in pen and had "ghetto girl" written over it. Police weren't sure what to make of it, and asked for anyone who knew anything about the business card to come forward.

As the letter about Tabitha was being passed out, the students as a whole seemed to be rather subdued. Some even felt frightened as they glanced over the contents. It opened up a dialogue about Tabitha and why she was still missing, and it seemed to help her classmates to be able to talk about her. They were encouraged to discuss the letter with their parents and to report any information they might have even if it seemed insignificant to them.

Shortly after the letter had been sent home with students, police finally got the answer they had been seeking about the business card found in Tabitha's room. The card had been printed up as a joke by one of Tabitha's friends, with assistance from Tabitha herself. It had nothing to do with the disappearance at all, it had simply been made by two young girls experimenting with a home printer. Tabitha's friend hadn't known police were even aware of the business card; police had never released any information about it to the public. Had she known, she would have solved the mystery for them months earlier.

On August 19th, an 11-year-old girl in Northport, Alabama went missing under circumstances eerily similar to those in Tabitha's case. Heaven "Shae" Ross, who resembled Tabitha in appearance, went missing while walking to her school bus stop that morning. Her 13-year-old sister was already at the bus stop waiting for her and became concerned when she didn't show up. Police were called within 30 minutes of the child's disappearance, but detectives there had been unable to come up with any solid leads. Bo and Debra made a rare trip away from home to go to Alabama and offer their support to the Ross family. Sadly, Shae's body would be discovered a few months later. Her murder remains unsolved.

In October, some of Tabitha's classmates marked the sixth month anniversary of her disappearance with music: along with one of their teachers, they wrote and recorded a song for Tabitha called "Come Home." They performed their song for the first time at a candlelight vigil held at Bailey Middle School. Despite the rainy weather, around 150 people came out to show their support for Tabitha's family, many of them wearing purple ribbons pinned to their shirts. The students later produced a CD with "Come Home" on it. They sold copies of the CD for $5.00, donating all the money they made to the reward fund.

In December, the Tuders appeared on the Montel Williams Show, along with several other families with missing loved ones. Well-known psychic Sylvia Brown offered her thoughts on each of the cases but offered little in the way of comfort. She told Bo and Debra their daughter was dead, then gave them more specific information concerning locations and names that she believed were relevant to the case. This information was passed on to police, and though they didn't believe any of it, they checked into the locations mentioned. They found nothing to indicate any of the information provided was at all relevant to Tabitha's case, which was a relief for Debra. She refused to believe that her daughter was dead and said she would continue to feel that way unless Tabitha's body was found.

The new year meant a new police chief in Nashville. The job went to Ronal Serpas, and he told the media that Tabitha's case was the Metro Police Department's number one priority. He firmly believed that the missing teenager had not left voluntarily, giving Tabitha's family a power ally that they had lacked when Deborah Faulkner had been the acting police chief. Faulkner had hoped she would be offered the position permanently, and many believed that the way in which she had handled Tabitha's case had been the main reason why she didn't get the job.

A public celebration marking Tabitha's 14th birthday was held on February 15, 2004. Family, friends, classmates, and even members of law enforcement gathered at Bailey Middle School, where a brief prayer service was held. Following the service, the crowd released

14 balloons into the air and planted a pink flowering cherry tree in Tabitha's honor. Normally, the teen would have celebrated her birthday at home with a cookout, and her family decided to keep up the tradition. They bought a pink and white birthday cake, and Bo grilled hot dogs and hamburgers as he always did. Bo said he knew Tabitha was still alive, they just didn't know where yet. Friends and family shared happy memories about her as they ate, all of them hoping that this would be the first and only time they had to celebrate her birthday without her.

On the first anniversary of Tabitha's disappearance, her family held a "Continue the Search" walk, inviting the public to join them as they traced over the last steps Tabitha had taken before vanishing. They gathered at 7:45 am, then made the two-block walk to the bus stop. The short journey had a surreal feeling; it still didn't seem possible that the energetic teenager could go missing on such a short walk, just a few steps away from the safety of her bus stop.

When the investigation first started, detectives were receiving more than 50 tips a day about the missing girl. A year later, this had slowed to a trickle of only five or six tips a month. While it was still considered an active investigation, detectives were running out of leads to follow. Knowing that they needed to keep Tabitha's picture out there to ensure the public didn't forget she was missing, her family created "Team Tabitha." The teen had adored going to the Saturday night car races at Highland Rim Speedway with her parents. Her brother, Kevin, was one of the race car drivers, and he had loved seeing his little sister there to cheer him on. Now, he and three other drivers – Team Tabitha – had large pictures of Tabitha mounted on the hoods of their race cars. They raced the cars every Saturday night, and the racetrack would announce the phone number for the tip line before their races. They were hopeful that this might bring in the tip they needed to crack the case. The racetrack held a special "Race for Tabitha" day, where they raised around $1100 to contribute to the reward fund. They also kept information about her case on their own website, encouraging people to go to police with any information they might have.

Despite their persistence, the family headed into the second holiday season without Tabitha – and without any answers. They were still in shock that she had managed to disappear without a trace, and the thought of spending every holiday for the rest of their lives without her was simply too much to bear. Debra had bought presents for Tabitha the first Christmas she was missing and had wrapped them and placed them under the tree. This year, she couldn't bring herself to go shopping for gifts at all, though Tabitha's favorite snack – a Slim Jim and a Dr. Pepper – was set out just in case. Bo had gone to the grocery store and gotten all the ingredients for chili pie, Tabitha's favorite meal, as well.

Although they didn't do as much decorating as usual, they did put up a Christmas tree. The angel tree topper was wearing a necklace with Tabitha's picture inside it. On an end table sat a small, lopsided tree that Tabitha had made. Fashioned out of coat hangers and adorned with tiny lights and tinsel, it had become one of their favorite decorations. Each year, they would carefully bring it out and give it a place of honor. It was a little piece of Tabitha, and it grew in importance as years passed slowly by, and Tabitha remained missing.

As time went by with no progress, Tabitha's case slipped out of the headlines. Eventually, it was reduced to a boilerplate article run once each year on the anniversary of her disappearance. The East Nashville neighborhood where the Tuders lived underwent a gradual change over the years, and the gentrification process brought new neighbors who had never heard of the missing girl. The little white house on Lillian Street remained the same, however, even as larger, cookie-cutter homes sprang up around it. The large vinyl banner with Tabitha's picture remained on the front porch, even if those walking by never met the young girl featured on it. Life went on around them, but the Tuders remained frozen in time, unable to move forward without knowing what had happened to their daughter.

Detectives still worked any leads that came in, and as the fifth anniversary of the disappearance grew near, they decided to work with the media to see if they could draw in any new tips. They asked the local newspapers and news stations to feature the case, and the media was more than happy to help. While there was no new information to report, they ran large articles rehashing the case from the beginning and included phone numbers for people to call if they had any information.

The media coverage did lead to a surge in tips, and detectives followed up on all of them. Many concerned angles that they had already pursued, but one lead appeared to be especially promising. In the years since Tabitha disappeared, one of her cousins had opened up a tattoo parlor. She was working there when a male customer made several interesting comments about the case. He claimed that he had been on Boscobel Street the morning Tabitha went missing, and he had seen her get into a car. His story was very similar to what the young boy at the bus stop claimed to see, with one significant difference: this man insisted the car was green, not red as the recent article had said. If true, this was a stunning revelation, but police were confused as to why the man had never bothered to come forward before. They took the lead as far as they could but were unable to find any information linking Tabitha and the car.

Around the seventh anniversary of the disappearance, the FBI announced that they were offering a $25,000 reward for information that would lead to finding Tabitha. They were hopeful that the large reward would be enough to entice anyone who had information to finally come forward. They firmly believed there were people who were withholding information, and they knew that money could be a very powerful motivator. Eight teams consisting of FBI agents and Metro police detectives also went door to door in the area, speaking with residents and handing out flyers with Tabitha's picture as well as the new reward information. An age-progression photograph of Tabitha was also released to give people an idea of what she might have looked like as a 20-year-old woman.

Despite the renewed push for information, Tabitha's case remained cold. Though there were still occasional sightings reported, Bo and Debra no longer got their hopes up when they heard about one. There had been a possible sighting reported in Nevada in 2010, and the girl looked so much like Tabitha that they family asked to have a DNA test done. Unfortunately, the test ruled the girl out. She was not Tabitha. In 2015, police received a tip that Tabitha was living in Nebraska. The information given over the phone sounded promising enough that investigators were sent to check it out, but they returned empty-handed. It would later be determined that the call had been a hoax, originating in a different country.

In April 2016, the FBI announced that they were doubling the reward offered in Tabitha's case. Unfortunately, not even the prospect of $50,000 was enough to bring in the information needed to solve the case.

Tabitha's case is still considered to be an open investigation, but police don't seem any closer to solving it than they were when she first went missing nearly 17 years ago. Though they faced criticism early on in the investigation, the department has a team of dedicated detectives and anyone who spent any amount of time working on the case would love nothing more than to see it resolved. Even now, rumors plague the investigation, and it's not easy to sort fact from fiction.

There is no one – friends, family, law enforcement – who believes that Tabitha ran off on her own. Even those who were convinced that was the case at first revised their opinion as time went by. Someone abducted Tabitha, the question, of course, is who. From the beginning, police did not believe the witness account of Tabitha getting into a red car, though their reason for discounting this tip is unclear. The 11-year-old boy who made the claim went to the same school as Tabitha, though he wasn't in the same grade, and he knew and liked her. Years later, Debra ran into this witness when he was in college. He stood by what he saw that day. Debra told a reporter "He told me he would never, ever get that out of his head. He said he saw what happened, and he kept apologizing that no one believed him. He said other kids [at school] would pick on him, but Tabitha never did. He said they were friends, and he would never make this up." Some people still believe that the man he saw was Jamie's boyfriend, and they believe that Jamie had somehow protected her boyfriend when he was interviewed by police. But the boyfriend passed a polygraph exam, even if Jamie did not. He also had an alibi for the morning in question, and it seems unlikely that he would have been able to kidnap Tabitha and then somehow get rid of her without anyone noticing he was gone. This doesn't mean that Tabitha didn't get into a red car, but Jamie's boyfriend wasn't driving that car.

Search dogs seemed to indicate that Tabitha had gotten into a car as well, and at a location that matches what the boy at the bus stop saw. Years later, someone would claim she had gotten into a green car, possibly a Mustang, with a decal of a snake on it. Police first learned of the green car after Tabitha had been missing for five years, and it was another eight years after that when a woman came forward claiming she suddenly remembered a man who drove a green car matching the description. Police were excited, as it was the first new lead in years, and quickly set about to find the man the woman told them about. His name was Juan, he had been a 19-year-old neighbor of the Tuders when Tabitha went missing. Because of his proximity, his name had come up in the investigation earlier, but there was no credible information linking him to the case, When detectives checked into the story this new witness told them in 2016, they realized that Juan still had no involvement in the case. The woman, for unknown reasons, had actually made up much of what she told them.

Unfortunately, the neighborhood where Tabitha lived was home to a host of unsavory characters, most of whom her parents had no idea about. In addition to registered sex offenders, there were several others who would later be arrested for crimes against young teens. Less than three weeks after Tabitha went missing, a man who lived five houses away from her was arrested for raping a minor at his home. He was caught when his own son walked in to find him assaulting a 16-year-old girl. His wife was also arrested, as she had been the one to force the girl to undress, telling her that her husband would not take no for an answer. There was nothing linking them to Tabitha, but it was unsettling to the Tuders, who had always assumed they were a nice, normal couple. It made them wonder how many others could be capable of the same kinds of acts.

There were numerous rumors that Tabitha had been taken and sold into the "Memphis Boys" prostitution ring. Early on, these rumors were so pervasive that Bo, Kevin, and a few family friends made the drive to Memphis and conducted their own investigation, interviewing prostitutes and trying to find anyone who may have seen Tabitha. They didn't learn any useful information, and police cautioned them about putting themselves in danger like that again. Later, when there were rumors that Tabitha had been taken to Las Vegas, the group went there looking for her. They understood what they were doing was dangerous, but felt it was worth it if it brought them any closer to finding Tabitha. Unfortunately, they didn't learn anything on that trip, either.

Bo and Debra Tuders still reside in the same Lillian Street home Tabitha grew up in, and her bedroom still looks like it did when she last left. While they did consider moving, this is the only place Tabitha knew as home, and they decided they will stay there just in case she comes back.

Tabitha Danielle Tuders was just 13 years old when she went missing from Nashville, Tennessee in April 2004. She has blue eyes and blonde hair, and at the time of her disappearance, she was 5 feet tall and weighed 90 to 100 pounds. When last seen, she was wearing a pair of Mudd brand blue jeans, a light blue shirt, and white Reebok sneakers, and she was carrying her report card. If you have

220

any information regarding Tabitha, please call Metro Nashville Police Department Detective Steven Jolley at 615-862-7843.

Printed in Great Britain
by Amazon

35345645R00123